How to Find a Needle in a Haystack

Searching for a needle in a haystack is an important task in several contexts of data analysis and decision-making. Examples include identifying the insider threat within an organization, the prediction of failure in industrial production, or pinpointing the unique signature of a solo perpetrator, such as a school shooter or a lone wolf terrorist. It is a challenge different from that of identifying a rare event (e.g., a tsunami) or detecting anomalies because the "needle" is not easily distinguished from the haystack. This challenging context is imbued with particular difficulties, from the lack of sufficient data to train a machine learning model through the identification of the relevant features and up to the painful price of false alarms, which might cause us to question the relevance of machine learning solutions even if they perform well according to common performance criteria. In this book, Prof. Neuman approaches the problem of finding the needle by specifically focusing on the human factor, from solo perpetrators to insider threats. Providing for the first time a deep, critical, multidimensional, and methodological analysis of the challenge, the book offers data scientists and decision makers a deep scientific foundational approach combined with a pragmatic practical approach that may guide them in searching for a needle in a haystack.

How to Find a Needle in a Haystack
From the Insider Threat to Solo Perpetrators

Yair Neuman

CRC Press
Taylor & Francis Group
Boca Raton London New York

CRC Press is an imprint of the
Taylor & Francis Group, an **informa** business

First edition published 2023
by CRC Press
4 Park Square, Milton Park, Abingdon, Oxon, OX14 4RN

and by CRC Press
6000 Broken Sound Parkway NW, Suite 300, Boca Raton, FL 33487-2742

© 2023 Yair Neuman

CRC Press is an imprint of Taylor & Francis Group, LLC

Library of Congress Cataloging-in-Publication Data

Names: Neuman, Yair, 1968- author.
Title: How to find a needle in a haystack : from the insider threat to solo
    perpetrators / Professor Yair Neuman.
Description: Boca Raton : CRC Press, 2022. | Includes bibliographical references
    and index. | Summary: "Searching for a needle in a haystack is an important
    task in several contexts of data analysis and decision-making. Examples include
    identifying the insider threat within an organization, the prediction of failure in
    industrial production or pinpointing the unique signature of a solo perpetrator,
    such as school shooter or a lone wolf terrorist"— Provided by publisher.
Identifiers: LCCN 2022022647 | ISBN 9781032229768 (hbk) | ISBN
    9781032267234 (pbk) | ISBN 9781003289647 (ebk)
Subjects: LCSH: Criminal behavior, Prediction of—Methodology. | Criminals—
    Identification—Data processing. | Personality assessment—Data processing. |
    Psychology, Industrial—Data processing. | Threat (Psychology)
Classification: LCC HV6080 .N47 2022 | DDC 364.3—dc23/eng/20220706
LC record available at https://lccn.loc.gov/2022022647

ISBN: 978-1-032-22976-8 (hbk)
ISBN: 978-1-032-26723-4 (pbk)
ISBN: 978-1-003-28964-7 (ebk)

DOI: 10.1201/9781003289647

Typeset in Times
by KnowledgeWorks Global Ltd.

Contents

Acknowledgments

I would like to thank Irun Cohen for insightful discussions on the way our understanding of biological systems may inform our understanding of human systems; Roni Simons for deep and thought-provoking discussions on the way human psychology should be understood; Dan Vilenchik for fruitful collaborations on data science projects and for his critical and constructive reading of an earlier draft; Yochai Cohen, Eden Erez, Vlad Kozhukov, and Yoav Lev-Ran for research collaborations; Mike Fenton and Joshua Tschantret for their kind endorsements; Randi Cohen for her friendly editorial work and welcoming approach; Doron Bar-Shalom for enthusiastically supporting my creative ventures, and Hazel Bird for copyediting my book with expertise and respect for the text.

Preface

I have been involved, and am currently involved, as a PI, a chief scientist, and an adviser in cutting-edge projects sponsored by various agencies, including Israel's Ministry of Defense, the Intelligence Advanced Research Projects Activity (IARPA), the Defense Advanced Research Projects Agency (DARPA), a world-leading bank, and private companies. In my academic and non-academic projects, I've analyzed a variety of data, from medical records to financial data. What I've learned – and keep learning – from these projects is that data science is an art no less than a science, and that for real-world problem-solving, rather than academic research per se, there is a winning approach that provides us with a competitive edge. As a jack of all trades, it has come naturally to me to adopt this approach, which involves a struggle for deep scientific understanding, a multidisciplinary perspective, flexibility with no obligation to any dogma, and the uncompromising pursuit of real-world and creative engineering solutions by a *team* of dedicated and task-oriented people. This approach is expressed in this short book, which deals with a problem that repeatedly appears in certain challenging contexts: how to find a needle in a haystack. From delving into this problem, I have realized something that I might, with the benefit of hindsight, have expected: that the problem is much more complex and difficult to resolve than one might naïvely assume. This book introduces and analyzes some difficulties, solutions, and insights that popped into my mind as I faced the "needle challenge." The book should therefore be read more as a general approach to a problem than as a practical manual.

As this book may be highly relevant to a wide variety of readers, it is written in colloquial and friendly language that aims to be accessible to all. Whenever formulas and calculations appear, they are explained and presented in a way that any educated reader can understand. Moreover, the book is written from a highly personal approach as it emerged out of my experience, and it therefore reflects all the accompanying passion associated with exciting academic and non-academic challenges. Some of this personal experience involved the difficulties of an "armchair academic" painfully thrown into reality, and this has led me to feel deep respect for the challenges of the real world outside the academy, the practitioners who strive to address them, and the importance of technological "engineering" solutions that might be dismissed by highbrow academics but nevertheless are necessary for practical advancement. This book, which has been shaped by my personal experience, therefore involves an attempt to gain a deep scientific understanding, but one attuned to engineering solutions. While inevitably tied to the seriousness of a scientific and engineering approach, the style of the book is friendly and combines professional seriousness with humor (which is a necessary ingredient for cognitive flexibility). The book is also highly critical, as critique, in the sense of what may be described as *evaluative reflection*, is what allows us to improve our solutions by reflecting, evaluating, analyzing shortcomings, and proposing improvements.

One final word should be said about the potential sensitivity of the topic. I once submitted a paper about the automatic identification of vengeful themes in textual data to an academic journal. The editor responded saying that, given the "sensitivity" of the subject, the journal was not comfortable sending the paper for review and wanted to discuss with me some concerns relating to "overgeneralization." The paper involved four datasets, respectively, containing texts by Islamic terrorists, right-wing terrorists, school shooters, and content mined from discussion groups dealing with revenge. Such "sensitivity" to the delicate feelings of people ranging from bloody murderers in the name of Allah or white supremacy to those who giggle about revenge porn served to painfully sharpen my awareness of the current Zeitgeist (i.e. the intellectual and cultural climate of the era) prevalent among some circles.[1] There is no need to mention my response to the sensitive editor, and the paper was immediately withdrawn. However, I'm aware that in this Zeitgeist, the (human) needle challenge might be misinterpreted by some ideologically biased critiques as a guide to manhunting. I've repeatedly confronted (mostly zealous) academics and "intellectuals" who confuse technology for evil. In one talk, given at an Israeli university, I was even criticized by a faculty member from the field of social studies of science for presenting pedophile-screening technology developed by the participants at the CLEF 12 conference. The anxiety associated with the technological Big Brother was far more pressing to this "critical" faculty member than the anxiety associated with sexual predators seeking their young victims. My first objection to such a critique, whether simply naïve or ideologically inclined, is that technology is merely a tool, just like a knife, a fire, or nuclear energy. Technology is indifferent to its use. It simply shows us how to do things better. Given this indifference, the development of potentially harmful technologies should be done from a clear moral stance and by understanding the constructive scope of the technology, its shortcomings, and its potentially negative side effects and consequences. The moral stance that I adopt in my work and in this book stands for the right of just and open societies to defend themselves while taking all precautionary steps to prevent the misuse of their technologies. Despite all of the inevitable difficulties that accompany this stance, it is the perspective from which I consider threats such as lone wolf terrorists and school shooters as legitimate targets. By definition, this book doesn't address a certain academic audience from the humanities and social sciences. Those academics who have a different perspective may feel uncomfortable reading this book, but many others will hopefully find it thought provoking and relevant to addressing the practical aspects of the needle challenge.

Yair Neuman
Israel

NOTE

1. For a humorous and artistic expression of this Zeitgeist, see the comedy drama *The Chair* (2021).

The Needle Challenge

1

From Shipping Vessels to the Insider Threat

Each year, millions of shipping containers enter US ports.[1] These containers are mostly innocent boxes used to ship an enormous variety of products, from bananas to books. However, some of them might hide things less innocent than bananas. For example, they may be used to smuggle illegal substances, such as drugs. In 2020, the *Wall Street Journal* reported that "seizures of cocaine aboard commercial ships and private vessels world-wide more than tripled over the past three years, to *73.2 metric* tons in 2019" (Paris, 2020, my emphasis). While the reported number of seizures may be interpreted as indicating the increasing success of law enforcement agencies, it is no less indicative of the increased use of shipping containers to smuggle drugs.

Using containers to smuggle drugs seems to be an excellent strategy given the high-street price of drugs and the extremely low chance of law enforcement agencies finding them in a container. In the USA, the street price of a gram of cocaine is $120 (Statista, 2021). Ten kilograms of cocaine, a weight equivalent to a single barbell used by a teenager to develop his biceps, might be sold on the streets of New York for $1.2 million (tax free, needless to say). The motivation to smuggle drugs is therefore clear and so is the choice to use shipping containers. While the ideal of the US government is to inspect all inbound containers, the actual percentage is extremely low – reported in 2016 to be around 4% (Hans, 2016). Given the size of a modern shipping vessel, searching it for drugs is like searching for a needle in a haystack. Streetwise drug dealers know their statistics better than others ….

DOI: 10.1201/9781003289647-1

While drugs are definitely a problem, even greater concerns exist with regard to the smuggling of weapons, specifically those of mass destruction: chemical, biological, radiological, or nuclear. Since September 11, 2001, the USA has been extremely concerned about a scenario where a dirty (or even non-dirty) bomb might enter the country and be used for a mega-terror attack. This scenario may sound apocalyptic, which it is, and we find it difficult to imagine that it could happen. However, history teaches us that governments and intelligence agencies alike have repeatedly been prone to what we might term failures of imagination. While the smuggling of a dirty bomb into the USA may seem unimaginable, it is definitely a *possible* scenario for which the USA should be prepared. Like tsunamis, rare and catastrophic events – whether real or imagined – should not be dismissed.

While advances in technology have improved the screening and imaging of shipping containers, it is impossible to screen each and every container for each and every illegal material and object. The perfect screening procedure would entail a bottleneck in the supply chain, which would be extremely costly both in money and time. The situation is even more challenging where small vessels are concerned. In the USA, there were 11.84 million registered vessels in 2020 (Statista, n.d.). A small vessel cannot be automatically screened, and smuggling drugs in a recreational yacht returning from Mexico seems to be a risk that dealers believe it is worth taking. This threat from small vessels was in fact described in 2008 by US Coast Guard admiral Thad Allen (2008) as a "needle in a haystack" problem, because searching such a huge number of vessels to identify threats seems to be mission impossible.

There are many other problems – beyond screening containers and small vessels – that can be described in terms of searching for a needle in a haystack. Consider another one, which is that of the *insider threat*. The insider threat is defined as:

> The potential for an insider to use their authorized access or understanding of an organization to harm that organization. This harm can include malicious, complacent, or unintentional acts that negatively affect the integrity, confidentiality, and availability of the organization, its data, personnel, or facilities.
>
> *(Cybersecurity & Infrastructure Security Agency, n.d.)*

As explained by Noonan (2018, p. 5), the insider threat is "a hard problem; there is no ground truth, innumerable variables, and sparse data. We often fail to acknowledge the impacts of socio-cultural and organizational influences on a person's capability, motivation, and opportunity to commit an insider crime." The insider threat is epitomized by the case of Edward Snowden. Snowden, an employee of the National Security Agency (NSA) and the Central Intelligence Agency (CIA), leaked an enormous number of classified documents. In his autobiography, Snowden (2019) justifies his behavior in moral ideological terms and presents himself as a heroic whistleblower. However, whether Snowden is a dirty traitor or a heroic whistleblower is a question that is beyond the scope of the current book.

While the NSA was clearly furious about the Snowden case (Levy, 2014), for the outsider, it is quite difficult to perform an objective *damage assessment* to better understand the impact of Snowden's leak on US national security. We don't know how many agents have lost their lives as a result of Snowden's leak, whether secret technologies have been exposed to foes and enabled them to adopt countermeasures, whether the leak entailed heavy financial consequences, or whether the threat to the reputation of the American intelligence community was as severe as has sometimes been reported. In contrast, in commercial companies, it is clear that insiders can cause considerable damage. The chief technology officer of a fintech company once said to me in a private conversation that his greatest fear was an employee stealing the company's intelligent algorithms. In private companies, employees cannot be screened in advance in the same way as employees within the intelligence community. Moreover, given privacy issues, they cannot be monitored in the same way as employees within the intelligence community. If one of them decides to accidentally or deliberately "share" the company's intellectual property, then the damage is enormous, with almost no tools available to prevent it in advance or even to prove the guilt of the insider beyond any reasonable doubt. In the old days, a traitor carrying a suitcase containing classified materials could have been tracked and targeted before they crossed enemy lines. However, in our current tech-oriented society, such scenarios reside only in memories of a dead past.

Back to the Snowden case. Unless they overreacted for some reason, we can take the responses of senior officials to the Snowden case to indicate that the damage he caused was a painful blow. However, the anxiety associated with the Snowden case does not only concern the damage already done. It is an anxiety that can also be projected into the future. In a big haystack – such as the NSA, with all of its subcontractors – there is always the potential that a needle is hiding that, despite careful clearance protocols, cannot be identified in advance or located in real time. The case of Snowden raises our awareness of the possibility that there are other insiders who currently operate under the radar, and this reasonable possibility is of great concern.

Both government agencies and private companies are founded on trust. If it does not trust its employees, an organization cannot properly function, and organizations such as the NSA make intensive efforts to ensure that those who work for them can be trusted. However, our psychological trust system has evolved in a totally different context from the one in which we are currently living. The Snowden case has likely led to a serious "trust issue" within organizations interested in keeping their secrets and this is deeply connected to the needle challenge, which itself is located in a broader cultural context. If a carefully selected and successful employee such as Snowden can be exposed as a traitor, then whom can we trust? Searching for an insider (threat) seems to be like searching for a needle in a haystack and for *a needle that doesn't necessarily exist*. This is why the insider threat invites a paranoid approach to security, albeit one with a very high toll that we cannot always pay.

In the context of the intelligence community, there only needs to be one needle for substantial damage to be caused for an organization, but such a needle is difficult if not impossible to find. In Israel, a recent mysterious case involved a former young intelligence officer from a classified technological unit who died in jail after being blamed for compromising national security. The Israeli Chief of the General Staff described the potential threat of the young officer in language that left no place for doubt: the insider, who didn't act for ideological reasons, could have caused serious damage, although this was luckily prevented in time (Wikipedia, 2022). Whether the success in preventing the damage was accidental or a result of an efficient screening system is not widely known. However, we do know that searching for an insider is like searching for a needle in a haystack, and in some contexts a failure to find the needle will have detrimental consequences. In the Israeli case, the needle was somehow identified, but the general lesson is clear, and the anxiety associated with this case can be projected to possible future insiders and the difficulty of identifying them in advance.

Let me now present a third example that may be discussed under the topic of finding a needle in a haystack; this example concerns solo perpetrators. Solo perpetrators are individuals who commit violent acts and who have no affiliation to any organization. They may be ideologically committed but don't operate as part of an organization or under a well-defined structure of command and control. School shooters are solo perpetrators. When they enter an educational institution (such as a high school or university) in order to shoot students and teachers, they usually do it on the basis of their own twisted motivation. A school shooter is not a part of a larger group of shooters. He (it is almost always "he") acts on his own and for his own disturbed psychological reasons. For example, Elliot Rodger, the perpetrator of the Isla Vista killings in 2014, was affiliated with the cyberculture known as "incel," which is focused around men who are unable to obtain romantic or sexual relations with women. However, his mass shooting was not launched by any "incel organization" but resulted from his own disturbed mind, envy, and misogynistic worldview.

A lone wolf terrorist is also a solo perpetrator. Some forms of terror are organization-based and even supported by governments. For example, the terror attack against US marines in Beirut in 1983 was launched by the terrorist organization Hezbollah, which is a proxy of the Iranian regime. However, a lone wolf is not sent by a government or an operative of a terrorist organization. For example, in 2016, an American citizen by the name of Omar Mateen shot to death 49 people and wounded 53 others. The mass murder took place in a gay nightclub in Florida where people were having fun shortly before the lone wolf arrived. It is reported that the murderer had been on the FBI's Terrorist Screening Database for some time (Wilber, 2016). During the period of the attack, this database is reported to have contained around 1 million names (Congressional Research Service, 2016). Finding the murderous needle in the haystack of candidates proved to be impossible. Even in a limited list of potential terrorists containing "only" 1 million individuals, it is likely that most of the individuals included in the list will not launch a terror attack and, if any are planning to launch an attack, they will probably not be identified in advance. Lone wolf terrorists have the potential to cause damage far beyond what has been caused by Mateen and his kind. Consider the following imaginary scenario and try to answer the question that follows it.

AN IMAGINARY SCENARIO

Dr. Adham Said is a 27-year-old British citizen of Egyptian origin. He is a bachelor and a loner who was raised in the UK, the country where he graduated with a Ph.D. in medical physics. Dr. Said holds a position in the radiation department at Queen Elizabeth Hospital, Birmingham. During recent years, Dr. Said has undergone a process of Islamic radicalization: he has started to regularly visit a mosque, has grown a beard, and attends meetings of people known as fundamentalists. Therefore, his name has been included in the watch list of the UK security agency MI5. On his Facebook page, Dr. Said expresses bitterness against "Western colonialism" and describes England as the land of the *kuffar* – those who do not believe in the existence of God. Moreover, he expresses despair about what he considers to be a total state of decadence and a sense of urgency that time is running out and that steps must be taken to prevent the world from falling apart. As a result of his work, Dr. Said has access to materials that could cause radioactive contamination (in the manner of the Goiânia accident of 1987).

    And now to the question: If Dr. Said decides to build a small dirty bomb to be used during rush hour on the London underground, what are the chances that he will be identified in advance? The answer you will probably give is that the chances are extremely low. Now, imagine that Dr. Said has a brother who is a biologist whose hobby is biohacking, as a result of which he has gained easy access to some cheap technologies sent from China through the mail. What are the chances that such an individual playing with some potentially nasty technologies would be identified in advance? Probably even lower than those of identifying his imaginary brother working at the hospital.

The three abovementioned cases that I have used to illustrate the situation of searching for a needle in a haystack – drug smuggling, intelligence leaks, and solo perpetrators – are negatively loaded. Why not use more positive examples, you may ask? After all, the needle is not necessarily a negatively loaded object, such as a bomb or a traitor. The needle could be a promising business opportunity, such as an underpriced company that may be a good investment. In this context, the needle is the company and the haystack is the enormous number of irrelevant companies in which the business opportunity hides.

The reason I have chosen to use negatively loaded examples is because this book is about *human needles* who seek to hide themselves – and for a good reason: they don't want to be found. Finding a needle in a haystack is therefore discussed in this book in a limited context: one where the needle is a human being and a negatively loaded "object" hiding in a haystack. Finding the needle is therefore important to avoid the damage that might be caused by this individual. This is the context where we find the insider threat, solo terrorists, and school shooters, and this context presents difficult challenges involving various issues, from psychological diagnosis to statistical modeling and decision-making.

At this point, you may be coming to understand that a needle in a haystack is not simply a rare event. A mega-earthquake is a rare event, the collapse of the stock market is a rare event, and so is a devastating tsunami. Predicting a rare event is a challenge that continues to be intensively addressed by scientists in various disciplines, from geology to economics. However, the difference between a tsunami and Snowden should be clear – Snowden is an *adaptive system* – and this difference invites a different approach. While a tsunami is indifferent to intensive scientific efforts to predict its appearance, an insider is not.

The more specific context in which I locate the discussion of the needle in a haystack is that of *data science*. From my modest experience, data science is not a science in the same way as physics or biology but a field that should combine deep *scientific* understanding of the modeled phenomena (i.e. domain expertise), *engineering* of a practical solution, and the *art* of creative contemplation necessary to address a serious challenge. In contrast with what some people believe, data science doesn't usually provide the silver bullet for a given problem. Analyzing data may expose temporal regularities, identify patterns, or provide a reasonable classification of objects; however, in itself, it does not provide *the* solution.

For instance, I have spent many hours with the chief IT officer of an international shipping company, discussing its problems and possible solutions. During the COVID-19 crisis, the company experienced a significant increase in cyberattacks. As I expected, I was able to identify that the Achilles' heel of the system was the human factor. Despite numerous training sessions and warnings, employees consistently violated security norms by opening suspicious emails, for instance, and exposing the system to phishing attempts, which can be more than enough for a sophisticated cybercrime organization seeking a ransom or trying to steal information and money. During a discussion of the possibility of using data science to identify sloppy employees in order to reduce the number of successful phishing attacks, the officer explained to me that such technology would be irrelevant for two reasons. First, the percentage of sloppy employees was so high that in the real world, where perfect employees cannot easily be found, there will always be someone who opens the organization's door to a cyberattack. Second, he argued, it might be possible to identify sloppy employees, but no worthwhile actions could be derived from doing so. For instance, sending a warning signal to the system administrator that an employee has violated a security protocol would be of no use given the enormous number of alarms (both correct and false) that would accompany such a system and the lack of sufficient cybersecurity personnel to determine whether a warning signal deserved careful attention. He was definitely right. Automatically identifying sloppy employees would be nice, but too many employees are vulnerable to social engineering attacks and therefore marking them as potential entrance points for outsiders cannot easily be translated into appropriate preventive steps. Without connecting data science with the science of practically doing the right thing, data science – with all of its buzzwords – is irrelevant. One possibility could have been to introduce a "reinforcement system" whereby identified sloppy employees were fined for violating the security protocol. This sounds like a simple derivative of the so-called Pottery Barn rule: "you break it, you buy it." In other words, if you break the security protocol, you should pay for this violation in order to prevent you from making the same mistake again. Reasonable as this proposal may sound, finding conscientious employees is always a challenge, and creating disgruntled employees – specifically through the decisions of an automated system with a high level of false positives (i.e. false alarms) – would be likely to backfire against the very logic that motivated this strategy.

Here is another example of the possible shortcomings of data science when it is not associated with the relevant deeds. A couple of years ago, I gave a keynote talk about my work. While I took a break after the talk, I was approached by a person who presented himself as working for one of the European governments. He told me that the technologies I'd presented for identifying the signature of solo perpetrators were interesting but that the country's government faced a problem that was different from that of how to *classify* perpetrators. Specifically, he mentioned ISIS jihadists returning home from fighting zones. These individuals have been involved in atrocities and have been marked by their respective governments as potential threats. The representative explained that his government knew exactly who these bad guys were and didn't need data science to mark them as threats. I agreed. The problem is not in identifying the bad guys but in picking out of the haystack (i.e. several hundred bad guys who have returned from ISIS fighting zones) the "needle" who is going to act. In other words, the challenge is to identify the threatening needles and arrest them before they decide to act. The issue is not just to determine the *signature* that characterizes the bad guys, although identifying the signature may be the first step, but also to examine *timing and acting*. As we cannot follow the footsteps of each and every jihadist returning home, we face a challenge, and, as in the cybersecurity example, this is a context where false alarms are problematic. Even if it resulted in the identification of a ticking bomb, arresting a former jihadist as a result of a red signal sent by an automatic system would inevitably lead to criticism. In Western democracies, preventive arrests are rare and considered to be illegitimate, just like mass surveillance of citizens or the violation of privacy. Arresting a former jihadist based on the say-so of an automatic system is difficult to justify, even if an excellent machine learning system suggests that there is a 90% chance that the jihadist is heading toward a violent act.

As you can see, in the real world, searching for a needle in a haystack and translating this search into *relevant actions* is much more challenging than might naïvely be thought from a data science perspective per se. Therefore, this book delves into the challenge of finding a needle in a haystack by adopting a complex, pragmatic, and modest approach. This has several implications: first, the constraints imposed by real-world situations requiring *action and intervention* must be taken into account when proposing practical data science tools; second, we must accept that a silver bullet that can fully address the needle challenge is probably not at hand; and, third, what is consequently required is a heterogeneous system of mechanisms – like our immune system – orchestrated so as to provide the optimal (rather than the ideal) actionable interventions.

MARTIAL ARTS IN THE REAL WORLD

At this juncture, several points should be made about the style of the book, already introduced in the preface. The book is self-contained and written in a friendly and mostly informal manner while focusing on conceptual understanding rather than on detailed formalities and technical issues. Saying that, the book heavily leans on ideas from science, statistics, and data science but, as said, presents them in a way that will hopefully be approachable for the non-expert. All technical concepts are explained to a degree where the book may be of interest and relevance even to those who have minimal knowledge.

Moreover, in addressing complex real-world challenges, a multi- and interdisciplinary approach is a must. Imagine a mission team formed by the NSA to design a post-Snowden protocol to prevent the next insider threat. Such a team would probably be composed of psychologists, who would be experts in analyzing Snowden's personality; experts in cybersecurity seeking new means of monitoring; the system's administrator, who would hold the keys to the system; intelligence experts, who would prioritize the secrecy of documents and access to them; and so on. However, without the ability to orchestrate such a team by *integrating* the different perspectives, going beyond specific and limited perspectives, such a venture would be destined to failure. This interdisciplinary approach is represented in this book, and I emphasize the idea of an *approach* because from my own perspective the approach is much more important than the technique (despite the fact that the latter will naturally often become the focus of a project).

The best metaphor for understanding this point is drawn from the martial arts. Traditional martial arts, such as karate, kung fu, and aikido, place heavy emphasis on technique and style. If you have ever observed martial arts displays, you may have noticed that they are highly similar to ballet performance with their emphasis on technique and finesse. Masters of aikido throw people into the air with grace and minimal effort; karate masters produce beautiful high kicks, hitting their targets with impressive precision; and masters of kung fu block their opponents' attacks using elegant forms poetically drawn from mythological animals (e.g. a blind dragon weaving its tail). However, if you are interested in the gap between theory and practice in the way I am, you may have noticed that people who make their living by fighting (e.g. mixed martial arts fighters or bouncers at nightclubs in Boston) seldom if ever use fancy blocks to avoid a punch and that, when they strike, you won't see grace or finesse. What characterizes these real-world "masters" is not the technique but the *approach or the attitude*, to include general principles such as timing, distance, and situational awareness. Remember this metaphor as I hope it will be developed in your mind as you read this book, leading you to understand the precedence of approach over techniques more fully.

NOTE

1. The estimated number in 2016 was 12 million (Hans, 2016).

REFERENCES

Allen, T. (2008). Friend or foe? Touch to tell. *The Lookout, XXXVIII*(4), 2–4.

Congressional Research Service. (2016). *The terrorist screening database: Background information*. Retrieved January 19, 2022, from https://www.everycrsreport.com/files/20160617_R44529_e24dca37574ac5bd794a0ce5333cab2cada5a306.pdf

Cybersecurity & Infrastructure Security Agency. (n.d.). *Defining insider threats*. CISA. Retrieved January 19, 2022, from https://www.cisa.gov/defining-insider-threats

Hans, G. (2016, August 24). *U.S. lawmakers say with new technology, it's time to inspect all inbound containers*. Westar. Retrieved January 19, 2022, from https://www.westarusa.com/u-s-lawmakers-say-new-technology-time-inspect-inbound-containers

Levy, S. (2014, January 13). *I spent two hours talking with the NSA's bigwigs: Here's what has them mad*. Wired. Retrieved January 19, 2022, from https://www.wired.com/2014/01/nsa-surveillance

Noonan, C. F. (2018). *Spy the lie: Detecting malicious insiders* (No. PNNL-SA-122655). Pacific Northwest National Laboratory. Retrieved January 19, 2022, from https://irp.fas.org/eprint/noonan.pdf

Paris, C. (2020, January 6). Global shipping faces troubling new smuggling questions. *Wall Street Journal*. Retrieved January 19, 2022, from https://www.wsj.com/articles/global-shipping-faces-troubling-new-smuggling-questions-11578330634

Snowden, E. (2019). *Permanent record*. New York, NY: Metropolitan Books.

Statista. (2021, June 25). *The street price of a gram of cocaine*. Retrieved January 19, 2022, from https://www.statista.com/chart/18527/cocaine-retail-steet-prices-in-selected-countries

Statista. (n.d.). *Number of registered recreational boating vessels in the U.S. from 1980 to 2020*. statista.com. Retrieved January 19, 2022, from https://www.statista.com/statistics/240634/registered-recreational-boating-vessels-in-the-us

Wikipedia. (2022). *Tomer Eiges*. Retrieved January 19, 2022, from https://en.wikipedia.org/wiki/Tomer_Eiges

Wilber, D. Q. (2016, June 12). Omar Mateen was taken off a terrorist watch list, but keeping him on it wouldn't have stopped him from buying guns. *Los Angeles Times*. Retrieved January 19, 2022, from https://www.latimes.com/nation/la-na-orlando-nightclub-shooting-live-omar-mateen-was-taken-off-a-terrorist-1465772737-htmlstory.html

What Is a Needle in a Haystack?

2

A Lesson from Miss Lucy and Vladimir Putin

"Needle in a haystack" is a commonly used idiom whose applications range from quantum search applications for unsorted data to the surveillance of mosquito-borne arboviruses. Given the extensive use of the phrase, it is not surprising that it has perhaps become a bit of a cliché, losing its informative value. In this context, it is highly important to clarify the meaning of the phrase in such a way that it may be effectively used as a guiding light to address real-world challenges.

In all of the example applications of the phrase in Chapter 1, it is used to describe something, be it a virus or a perpetrator, that is extremely difficult or impossible to locate. The reason for the difficulty in locating the object is that "it is *hidden* among … many *other* things" (*Oxford English Dictionary*, my emphasis). Therefore, we have a situation where we are searching for an object (i.e. seeking to locate it), and the object is hidden in a noisy environment – that is, an environment containing many other objects that are similar to the object to a degree where they cannot easily be distinguished, and the object cannot easily be recognized. As you can see, searching for the needle is a challenge that involves both *localization* and *recognition* (an important point discussed in Chapter 7).

Contrary to what might be implied by describing the needle as "rare," the size of the haystack is not necessarily huge. In a small haystack of several

DOI: 10.1201/9781003289647-2

hundred returning jihadists, there may be a needle planning to continue his jihad on European soil. Rarity is therefore a relative concept that does not precisely tell us the size of the haystack.

In sum, first, we have an object that is *rare*. Second, the object is hidden. It is concealed rather than evident, and it is concealed among other things in a way that makes it difficult to *recognize* it. For example, in *Enter the Dragon*, one of the most successful action movies ever made, there is a memorable concluding scene where the hero, the legendary Bruce Lee, is fighting a crime lord by the name of Han. The fight takes place in Han's palace and more specifically in a room full of mirrors. It has been reported that 8,000 mirrors were used for this iconic scene (Quizzclub, n.d.), in which the image of the bad guy is reflected in the mirrors and the hero tries to locate the needle (i.e. Han) in the haystack of his numerous reflections.

It is highly important to emphasize that the needle cannot be easily distinguished from the stalks of hay in the haystack. The needle in the haystack is both rare *and* (almost) indistinguishable, at least during the first phase of the search process. However, this point is not always well understood. Some rare events can be identified easily, which means that being rare has nothing to do with the difficulty of recognition. For example, heterochromia iridum (Scientific American, 2001) is a condition with an incidence of 1 in 200,000 where people have eyes of different colors. It is rare but easily identified. To put this differently, rarity cannot be identified with the difficulty of recognition. A rare object or phenomenon may be difficult to predict but we must clearly differentiate between prediction and recognition/diagnosis. Some rare objects and phenomena are easy to recognize.

At this point, you may ask whether the needle challenge can be reduced to that of *anomaly detection*. In data science, anomaly detection "is the identification of rare items, events or observations which raise suspicions by *differing significantly from the majority of the data*" (Wikipedia, 2022, my emphasis). Anomaly detection can also be defined as the process of "identifying unexpected items or events ... which *differ from the norm*" (Goldstein & Uchida, 2016, my emphasis). The main emphasis of anomaly detection is therefore on some kind of deviation from a norm or a pattern that it is not necessarily difficult to identify. For instance, if a positive correlation or association exists between height and weight, then a 25-year-old man whose height is 160 cm and whose weight is 160 kg may easily be identified as an anomaly. We know the norm and can easily recognize this anomaly. To the reader who is familiar with the field of anomaly detection, it must be emphasized that the needle is an anomaly but that this human anomaly is very different from the anomalies usually discussed in anomaly detection. As will be explained, searching for the "needle anomaly" entails searching for an adaptive object just before it becomes an "anomaly," all while the object is seeking to hide its anomalous status. These points will be fully elaborated, but at this point, the reader should keep in mind that the needle anomaly is quite different from common anomaly detection, although the needle in its final identified form may be considered an anomaly.

Let me further illustrate the basic idea of anomaly detection in the context of *supervised* fraud detection. A supervised machine learning (ML) algorithm learns by using labeled cases. For example, a credit card company might label an enormous number of transactions using two tags only: fraud and non-fraud. Each transaction is accompanied by a list of *features* (i.e. measurable variables) that classify it into one of the two relevant classes (i.e. fraud and non-fraud). The ML algorithm learns the best discriminatory function to categorize transactions as fraud or non-fraud and, if it is successful, may be used to identify novel instances as frauds.

For instance, let's assume that Miss Lucy is a 90-year-old lady from Austin, Texas. The history of her previous purchases is translated into content categories (e.g. food, electronics, medicine) and an anomaly is defined as a significant deviation from her past pattern of purchases. In fact, by learning such a pattern of deviation from a labeled dataset, a supervised ML algorithm such as Naïve Bayes may successfully use the feature of "deviation from past purchases" as a warning signal. If the algorithm notices that on Saturday night the 90-year-old Miss Lucy appears to be purchasing a pair of 20 kg dumbbells, an Italian shaving foam, and a luxurious sports watch, then it may signal that a fraud is taking place and that there is a high probability that poor Miss Lucy's credit card information has been stolen.

Anomaly detection seems to be intuitive to understand: (1) something strange (i.e. different from the norm) is happening, (2) we don't like it, and (3) we must do something about it. The idea of something being "strange" is an anomaly tag that is highly informative with regard to a well-defined criterion. Think, for example, about shell companies. Although in themselves shell companies are legal and not necessarily illegitimate entities, they can be used for illegitimate purposes, such as money laundering and kleptocracy. The Panama Papers and Pandora Papers leaks exposed a network of hidden corruption that uses shell companies. Now, let's imagine that an Eastern European crime organization is collaborating with a Middle Eastern terrorist organization that is making its living through dealing drugs. The terrorist organization is laundering its dirty money using a company owned by its Eastern European friends. This is actually a holding company that manages, among several other assets, a successful porn site going by the name Adult Entertainment Ltd. Now, it is quite sensitive to track the money paid by the enthusiastic subscribers to a porn site, and Adult Entertainment Ltd. can therefore easily be used to launder the money arriving from the Middle Eastern drug dealers. The company is not a real company that employs workers or makes money, but a cover story used to launder the money of drug dealers through a porn site. In fact, Adult Entertainment Ltd. may be part of a bigger spider's web of companies and one of them may even support the Society for Islamic Justice, Freedom and Redemption. This (imaginary) society may support people and ideas affiliated with the terrorist organization while carefully hiding any link to the dirty money and its source.

In order to identify Adult Entertainment Ltd. as a shell company, we might use anomaly detection technologies. For instance, if the company is registered in a place where the owners are not required to be disclosed, then this is a warning signal. Moreover, we can use Google Maps to locate the exact address of the company. If we notice that the company is located in a side alley in Karachi, Pakistan, and in an office with no reported use of electricity, this may seem like an anomaly that it is worth checking out. Many years ago, I visited what seemed to be a respected small tech company. When I arrived at the place, I noticed that its office was located in a small building. The most prominent office neighboring the tech company was one offering "Thai massage." When I entered the office, I immediately noticed that dust was covering the shelves. This was a shell company that, despite its impressive internet site, was hiding something else.

While the idea of an anomaly seems to be easy to understand, it is argued that "despite abundant research and valuable progress, the field of anomaly detection cannot claim maturity yet. It lacks an overall, integrative framework *to understand the nature and different manifestations of its focal concept, the anomaly*" (Foorthuis, 2021, p. 298, my emphasis). Conceptual difficulties are always interesting as they urge us to better clarify the meanings of the concepts we use and to be precise about the appropriate contexts for using them. For instance, the platypus is an Australian creature tagged as belonging to the class of Mammalia, the same class to which we human beings belong. However, the platypus is considered to be an anomaly as it is an egg-laying creature, like birds and reptiles. It may be an interesting philosophical question whether this is a "real" anomaly or whether it was formed through the shortcomings and rigidity of our classification system. After all, the platypus is real, and if there is an anomaly then it is arguably an anomaly of our schemes rather than an anomaly of nature. As philosophical discussions are beyond the scope of the current book, I would urge you to consider what is the specific *action-motivated context* in which it is relevant to ask whether the platypus is a mammal or not. In other words, what is the "difference that makes a difference" (Bateson, 1972/2000)? With such an approach in mind, we may avoid the useless path of philosophical rumination in favor of a more pragmatic approach. Saying that, I do not mean that conceptual clarifications are useless. On the contrary, conceptual analysis is highly important as long as it is done within the appropriate context and not in and for itself. For example, defining an anomaly as a deviation from a norm might be problematic in some practical contexts, specifically where labeled data is not available for a supervised ML anomaly detection algorithm.

Understanding this shortcoming may lead us to seek other – more constructive – directions. For example, Isolation Forest is an unsupervised anomaly detection algorithm that proposes an interesting solution to the lack

TABLE 2.1   Estimated net worths of several political leaders

NAME	COUNTRY	NET WORTH (USD)
Vladimir Putin	Russia	70 billion
Mario Draghi	Italy	50 million
Angela Merkel	Germany	12 million
Justin Trudeau	Canada	10 million
Joe Biden	USA	9 million
Boris Johnson	England	4 million
Emmanuel Macron	France	1 million

Source: Data from https://www.celebritynetworth.com

of labeled data and the need to refer to some norm. The algorithm recognizes that anomalies are "few and different" (Liu, Ting, & Zhou, 2008, p. 1) and, instead of looking for a deviation from a norm, seeks to identify the unique features of the anomalies. Let's explain this by using a specific example. In Table 2.1, you will find a partial list of political leaders and their reported respective net worth. The list was prepared in July 2021, before the elections in Germany, but the point may be clear even if the data are not fully up to date. Figure 2.1 presents the same information on a logarithmic scale.

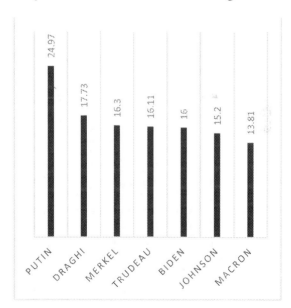

FIGURE 2.1   The estimated net worths of the politicians listed in Table 2.1 on a logarithmic scale.

There is no need for sophisticated methodologies to identify who is the anomaly, as eyeballing Figure 2.1 is enough. The estimated net worth of Vladimir Putin is on a scale totally different from that of the rest of the leaders, a fact that can be simply explained by the generous salary paid to the Russian president by his people.

Let us now use this data to explain the Isolation Forest approach. The decision tree in Figure 2.2 uses one feature only (net worth) and aims to identify each leader in our small dataset. As you can see, Putin is located at the top of the tree, while Boris Johnson and Emmanuel Macron are found at the bottom. The Isolation Forest suggests that if we build an *ensemble of decision-tress* for a given dataset, then the anomalies are those instances that have the *shortest average path lengths* on the trees. This unsupervised anomaly detection algorithm takes a non-standard approach to anomaly detection by suggesting that instead of looking for a simple deviation from a norm, we should do something else.

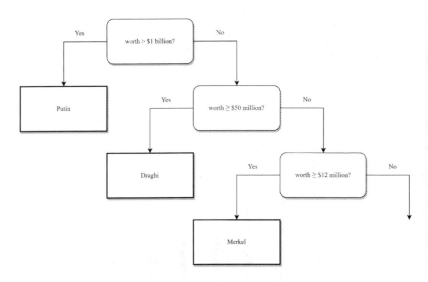

FIGURE 2.2   A partial decision tree using the net worth figures in Table 2.1.

Notice that by using the feature of *gender*, Merkel could have emerged as an anomaly by being the only woman in the list. Different features would result in different anomalies, meaning that the search for anomalies is context dependent and meaningful only with regard to a particular well-defined criterion. For example, in a case where we would like to identify signs of corruption, net worth may be a relevant feature. However, in a case where we would like to learn about equal opportunities, gender may be a relevant feature.

At this point, we may recall Wittgenstein's ruler: "Unless you have confidence in the ruler's reliability, if you use a ruler to measure a table you may also be using the table to measure the ruler" (Taleb, 2001, p. 224). In the context of anomaly detection, this means that if your device for detecting anomalies is used for the same set of data and identifies different anomalies in different contexts, then your basic notion of an anomaly is context dependent. This is trivial but worth mentioning.

Detecting anomalies, however, is quite different from addressing the needle challenge. By definition, an anomaly is distinguishable, whereas the needle in the haystack is not. The needle is different from the stalks of hay but cannot be easily distinguished from them because in most salient aspects it is more similar to the stalks than different from them. The distinguishing features are contextual and difficult to identify, and the useful distinguishing features are not those clearly observed but those that lead to the *formation* of the needle. Let me explain this important point using two examples.

Ted Bundy, a notorious serial killer, was an anomaly in terms of his deviation from social norms. After all, the overwhelming majority of people do not find pleasure in murdering innocent young women. While Bundy's behavior was a clear anomaly, this anomalous behavior could not have been used in advance to recognize him among all individuals composing the haystack of suspects. From the perspective of the outcome, Bundy was a clear *qualitative* anomaly (i.e. being a serial killer), but this anomaly could only be known post hoc. What we are interested in are the *quantitative*, multivariate, and under-the-radar attributes that could have signaled Bundy as a potential needle in the haystack of suspects in order to better identify him as the murderer. The same line of reasoning holds for the above example concerning political leaders, where we saw how Putin can easily be identified as an anomaly using Isolation Forest.

However, finding Putin in a haystack of people may not be a very interesting task, just as identifying the convicted Bundy as an anomaly is not an interesting task. As explained by Reeves and colleagues (2021), the "competitive edge" lies not in identifying an existing anomaly but in identifying an *evolving* anomaly just before it reaches maturity. Here we get into one of the major potential fallacies of the needle challenge: the confusion between the salient and the hidden. Let me explain this point, drawing on *Wind from the Sea*, a famous 1947 painting by Andrew Wyeth. The painting presents the inside view of a window as the wind blows in and moves the curtains. The wind coming from the sea, being the hero of the painting, cannot be seen. We reason about its existence from the tattered curtains. The wind is the cause of the *observed* moving curtains. While the observable is simple to recognize, the real force behind it is the unobservable wind from the sea, whose existence is inferred. The needle challenge urges us to move from simple observables to the unobservable, which is the real informative factor we are seeking to find.

Let me further elaborate this point using the case of Vladimir Putin, Edward Snowden's current patron (see Chapter 1 for more on Snowden). Recall Boris Yeltsin, president of Russia from 1991 to 1999, and imagine the American intelligence community closely observing the last days of this alcoholic president, who was the leader of a nuclear superpower. The intelligence community might have asked itself who was the candidate who aspired to replace the declining president. The needle-in-the-haystack problem would have been to identify his successor, which as we now know was Putin, among those who made up the inner circle of the president. To gain a competitive edge in a task such as this, we need to identify weak and ambiguous signals indicating that a rare and almost indistinguishable object is appearing on our radar just a moment before the tipping point where the object becomes a distinguished anomaly. For such a challenging task, we should return to the idea of a needle that is both *rare* and (almost) *indistinguishable* and try to answer two basic and foundational questions:

1. How are rare events and objects formed?
2. What makes them difficult to recognize?

The following chapters attempt to answer these two foundational questions. Chapter 3 introduces the Galton machine as a model that explains how rare objects are formed. Through the idea of the Galton machine, the reader may better understand why the human needle is not a simple anomaly (e.g. fraud) of the kind discussed in anomaly detection. Moreover, the Galton machine may be used as a model to explain how needles are *dynamically* formed. The dynamic aspect of the needle's formation is highly important in addressing the needle challenge, and the Galton machine can be used to model this dynamic aspect. Then, Chapter 4 explains what makes needles difficult to identify by asking whether I am a psychopath and explaining how this example points to the problem of false positives. Subsequently, Chapter 5 explains through the Galton Machine why it is inherently difficult to identify a needle in a haystack, Chapter 6 explains the binary fallacy, which may mislead us in addressing the needle challenge, and Chapter 7 turns to the difference between localization and recognition.

REFERENCES

Bateson, G. (1972/2000). *Steps to an ecology of mind: Collected essays in anthropology, psychiatry, evolution, and epistemology.* Chicago, IL: University of Chicago Press.

Foorthuis, R. (2021). On the nature and types of anomalies: A review of deviations in data. *International Journal of Data Science and Analytics, 1–3512,* 297–331.

Goldstein, M., & Uchida, S. A. (2016). Comparative evaluation of unsupervised anomaly detection algorithms for multivariate data. *PLOS ONE, 11*(4), e0152173. doi: 10.1371/journal.pone.0152173.

Liu, F. T., Ting, K. M., & Zhou, Z. H. (2008, December). Isolation forest. In *2008 Eighth IEEE International Conference on Data Mining* (pp. 413–422). Los Alamitos, CA: IEEE Press.

Quizzclub. (n.d.). Roughly, how many mirrors were used in the fight scene at the end of the film "Enter the Dragon"? Retrieved January 19, 2022, from https://quizzclub. com/trivia/roughly-how-many-mirrors-were-used-in-the-fight-scene-at-the-end-of-the-film-enter-the-dragon/answer/599966

Reeves, M., Goodson, B., & Whitaker, K. (2021). The power of anomaly. *Harvard Business Review.* Retrieved January 19, 2022, from https://hbr.org/2021/07/the-power-of-anomaly.

Scientific American. (2001, November 3). How does someone get two different-colored eyes? Retrieved January 19, 2022, from https://www.scientificamerican.com/article/how-does-someone-get-two

Taleb, N. (2001). *Fooled by randomness: The hidden role of chance in life and in the markets.* New York, NY: Random House Incorporated.

Wikipedia. (2022). Anomaly detection. Retrieved January 19, 2022, from https://en.wikipedia.org/wiki/Anomaly_detection.

How Are Rare Events Formed?

3

Modeling through the Galton Machine

By definition, a rare event (or object) is an event (or object) whose frequency is relatively low by some standard. Winning a lottery is a rare event and so is dying in a shark attack (Sepulveda, 2021) or being struck by lightning (National Weather Service, n.d.). We can think about a rare object or a rare event by examining a *probability distribution*, which is just a fancy name for "the probabilities of occurrence of different possible outcomes" (Wikipedia, 2022b). If you are counting the two possible outcomes of a coin toss, then the probabilities of the outcomes (heads or tails) make up the probability distribution of the coin toss. Figure 3.1 shows a possible probability distribution describing the distribution of height among adult men. As you can see, height is normally distributed in the general population. This means that the distribution of the different outcomes (i.e. heights) is concentrated around the mean and the distribution is symmetric. The right side of the distribution is a mirror image of its left side. You may also notice that being taller or shorter than a certain height is a rare event. You will hardly ever meet adult men taller than 2 m or shorter than 1.5 m.

DOI: 10.1201/9781003289647-3

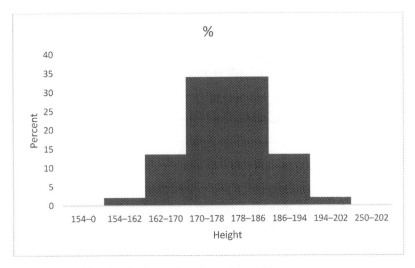

FIGURE 3.1   The distributions of adult men's height.

Source: Author.

There are different types of distribution, but, unless we are observing a flat, homogenous distribution in which the probabilities of all observations are the same, rare events can be found in all real-world distributions. For example, the distribution of scores on a measure of psychopathy is presented in Figure 3.2. As you can see, in this case, the distribution is not normal and only a few people score very high on the test, so scoring high on the psychopathy test is a rare event.

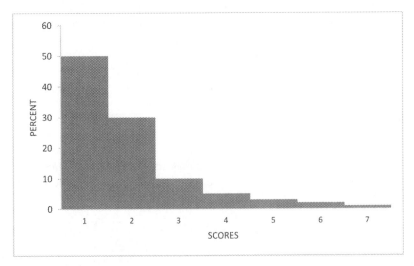

FIGURE 3.2   The distribution of psychopathy scores.

While rare objects and events can easily be located in a distribution, the way in which they are formed is not clear. We may wonder why rare events are rare, and to answer this question, we can turn to the explanation of how different distributions are formed in the first place.

The earliest and simplest explanation that I'm familiar with comes from the seminal work of Sir Francis Galton (1822–1911). As this explanation has the beauty of Occam's razor, I use it to explain the way rare events are formed.

Galton introduced a brilliant idea in which he modeled the way a normal distribution is formed. His idea is materialized in what is known as the Galton board, the bean machine, or the quincunx. We will examine it here in its material form, but I ask you to think of it from the beginning as an abstract machine as well (a point to be elaborated later). The machine is composed of rows of pegs, as shown in Figure 3.3. In each row, there is one or more peg, with the number of pegs corresponding with the row number: in the first row one peg, in the second row two pegs, and so on. Beads, beans, or balls are dropped from the top and whenever they hit a peg they bounce either to the left or to the right until they reach one of the number of bins (or baskets) located at the bottom of the machine. The bins collect the balls and the relative numbers of balls in each bin constitute the probability distribution.

FIGURE 3.3 The Galton machine.

Source: Wikimedia.

The bins at the bottom represent the different possible outcomes of the "experiment." If the probability of a ball bouncing to the right is the same as the probability of it bouncing to the left ($p = 0.5$), then, after a large enough number of rounds, we may surprisingly find that the distribution of the balls approaches the normal distribution. Figure 3.4 illustrates the formation of this normal distribution. This is a remarkable result, showing how the normal distribution may be formed by assuming *full ignorance* of the bouncing balls' behavior. As we have no way of knowing in advance which direction each ball may "chose," we assign equal probabilities to its choices. This is Laplace's principle of indifference (Wikipedia, 2022a).

FIGURE 3.4 The formation of the normal distribution.

Source: Wikimedia.

The result is that while we remain fully ignorant of the behavior of each *individual* ball and its final bin, on the *macro scale* – and over enough trials (i.e. dropping a large enough number of balls) – order is formed. For an outside observer, the behaviors of each individual ball could be attributed to the balls' free will, talent, and choices. For example, think of the balls as individuals and of the bins as categories of wealth, from very poor to very rich. When you observe an individual who is very rich, you may attribute their wealth to their talent. However, the Galton model urges us to consider the importance of pure chance in the outcome. Being highly rich can be attributed to talent, but how much of the wealth can be attributed to chance only? The Galton machine presents a remarkable result that it is not easy to intuitively understand. How can we explain this remarkable result in which, by assuming full ignorance, order is formed? Take a look at Figure 3.5, where the numbers represent the numbers of paths leading to each specific peg from the top node of the machine. What we are seeing in Figure 3.5 is actually Pascal's triangle, where the number on each peg is the sum of the numbers located above it. To understand the formation of the normal distribution, it is important to appreciate that those baskets with a higher frequency of balls are also those to which more paths converge.

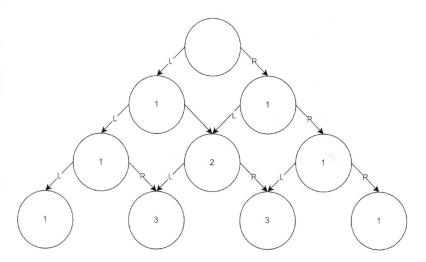

FIGURE 3.5   Trajectories on the Galton machine.

Source: Author.

Now think about each peg in more abstract terms as a crossroad in a decision tree where the subject (i.e. the ball) has to "decide" whether to turn right or left. This "decision" can be generalized to any other form of decision: the decision whether to marry this person (or not), the decision whether to study English literature or mechanical engineering, and so on. These choices should not necessarily be conceived as conscious and rational decisions; rather, it is more appropriate to think of them as binary *switches* channeling the direction of the individual balls. Such switches can be outside constraints. For example, being born to a family of a certain social class may be conceived as a binary switch with a high probability of directing you to the bin (or the outcome) of living as an individual of the same social class rather than as an individual of a different social class. A switch may be internal, such as where a genetic disease determines a person's life outcomes or where a personality trait directs the person to make specific life choices. Alternatively, it may be external, such as being born to a rich family.

The switches channel the balls into diverging and converging paths, leading to different outcomes. At this point, you will understand that we have moved from the material concretization of the Galton machine to its abstract form. To better understand this point, think about the evolution of human height. Various balls (i.e. individuals) are thrown into the system. Given a large enough number of evolutionary switches (e.g. genes, nutrition) that are independent of each other and practically ignorant – in the sense of having no preference for choosing one direction over another – the height of human beings may take the form of a normal distribution, as is actually observed (see Figure 3.1). By adopting this perspective, you may realize that rare events correspond with those bins or outcomes to which *fewer paths converge*, and common outcomes correspond with those to which *more paths converge*. The bins to which most paths converge are described in physics as "attractors." We can think of them as sinks channeling the flow of balls in a *phase space*, which is an abstract space in which all possible states of a system are represented. A normal behavior is an attractor to which several paths converge. A deviant form of behavior is a smaller region of the phase space at which a minority of the individual balls arrive. To repeat, "normal" and "deviant" are relative and contextual values. For an SS soldier during World War II, the mass murder of innocent children was a norm rather than a deviant behavior.

The structure of the Galton machine is the simplest way I can think of to model the formation of a distribution. It is a complete binary tree, a directed acyclic graph, which may not necessarily represent a complex system where cycles, feedback loops, and interactions exist between its composing units. However, scientific modeling prefers simplicity as long as the simplicity is justified by some reasonable criteria. We will stick to this approach while trying to get as much as we can from the Galton machine.

Modeled through the Galton machine, a deviant form of behavior (e.g. that of Ted Bundy; see Chapter 2) may be the result of two main factors. First, the more bins we have at the bottom of the machine, the more extreme (i.e. rare) the outliers will be. I find this conclusion to be very interesting. In a society where people can be "poor," "moderately wealthy," or "rich" (three categories or outcomes only), the Galton machine would lead to the distribution shown in Figure 3.6. In such a distribution, there are no rare events as it is quite common to be either poor or rich. However, if we increase the number of bins to four (i.e. "very poor," "somewhat poor," "somewhat rich," and "very rich"), then we may see that the percentage of rare cases (i.e. very poor or very rich) decreases to 12.5%. The deeper the tree – that is, the more variables, features, and switches are involved – the more complex the system is and so the more extreme and rare are the outliers.

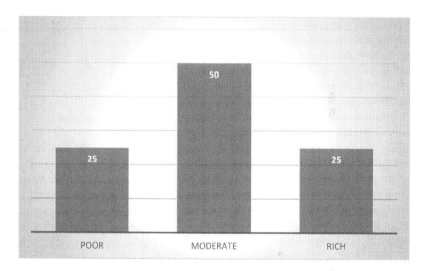

FIGURE 3.6   A histogram of wealth.

Source: Author.

The conclusion is that modeling the world with an increasing level of resolution seems to entail a complex world of sharper extremes, which inevitability will be more difficult to identify in the context of the needle challenge. From the complex systems perspective, this may be a trivial albeit important observation: the more complex our societies become, the sharper are the extremes. This conclusion may be an insightful observation for practitioners. In a world where there are different categories for insiders who commit a moral act (e.g. whistleblowers) and those who should be condemned (e.g. traitors), it is difficult to identify whistleblowers in advance. The mere existence of such a category, *by definition*, imposes constraints on our ability to identify the needle in the haystack (i.e. the traitor). This is a troubling conclusion for complex societies as it suggests that the seed of destruction, as expressed by extremes of all kinds, is a direct outcome of a system's complexity.

Another path to rarity doesn't have to involve a complex system. Think of a simple Galton machine where the probability of taking a right turn is 0.99 and the probability of taking a left turn is 0.01. In such a system, rare events are the result of biased probability in one direction, which results in a non-Gaussian distribution (i.e. a distribution that is not normal). Think, for example, about the rare event of having unusually high bone density, as depicted in the movie *Unbreakable* (2000). Having a high bone density may be the result of a *specific* genetic mutation (Boyden et al., 2002). If this is a kind of "dictator" gene that determines bone density, then there is no need for a complex explanation beyond what is provided by the rare genetic mutation. A simple Galton machine will suffice.

Given the two above explanations of how rare events are formed, we should ask ourselves whether human "needles" are rare objects that express a hidden underlying complexity or whether they are the result of a simple system with biased switches. Ted Bundy, the psychopath, could have been formed by a simple and currently unknown genetic mutation leading to an extreme expression of antisocial psychopathic personality disorder. In such a case, a simple blood test to identify the "psychopathic gene" would have been enough to reduce the size of the haystack of suspects and more easily find the Bundy among them. In contrast, Bundy's deviant personality could have emerged through a complex system of switches that, over the course of his development and life, led him along the rare path of maladaptive antisocial psychopathic personality disorder. We currently lack firm knowledge about the etiology (i.e. origin) of such disorders but may infer from our ignorance that the emergence of a psychopathic mind like Bundy's is probably the result of both a complex developmental machine and simple biased switches. We may further learn that becoming a rare object results from traveling along a *unique* path with switches that present highly biased choices. If someone is a child prodigy in classical music and can play Bach's *Goldberg Variations* at the age of three, they are likely to be a rare event that can mostly be attributed to unknown genetic switches, although the existence of an available piano (another switch) will be a necessary condition for the young genius to be recognized. In contrast, being a brilliant old novelist seems to follow the path of complexity. Regardless of the existence of a hypothetical genetic switch for writing talent, we can hardly imagine a great novelist decontextualized from their rich life experiences. Ernest Hemingway's novels cannot be imagined without his war experiences and Anton Chekhov's stories cannot be decontextualized from his travels across Russia.

Focusing on the *development* of rare objects is therefore highly important for the identification of needles. Anomaly detection algorithms focusing on the identification of anomalies have no theoretical ground for differentiating between *being* Putin and *becoming* Putin. They seek to identify or detect an object that already and by definition has the distinguishing mark of an anomaly. Such approaches use a bunch of measurable features (e.g. net worth) but assume that the features are present, and that beyond *features engineering* (e.g. the normalization of features) they should not be too much involved with the creative identification of weak signals indicating the approaching anomaly. The direction introduced through the above analysis suggests that instead of analyzing the final rare object per se (e.g. Bundy) with its accompanying set of characterizing features (e.g. killing young women), it is far more informative to try to *model* the path leading to the formation of the rare object. For example, instead of simply identifying the present mark of a jihadist acting as a lone wolf terrorist (a legitimate task in and of itself), we should focus on identifying switches – or *triggering events* – that may lead predisposed individuals to act in a violent manner. Such a triggering event may be, for example, a marital crisis leading to a tipping point of despair. While experiencing a marital crisis is not a discriminating feature that can informatively sort jihadists from non-jihadists, an etiologically oriented analysis may find it to be extremely relevant in a complex system that leads a *predisposed* individual to commit an act of terror. Moreover, being a Muslim is a distinguishing feature between being a jihadist or not. However, this is a poor feature as the overwhelming majority of Muslims are not jihadists. However, if we follow the line of reasoning presented so far, then when designing a screening system for jihadists, we may ask ourselves not only whether a subject is Muslim but also whether the subject has been Islamized, which might indicate a turning point in his life. A young French man who was Islamized in prison may be different from someone who was born and has lived his life as a Muslim. In other words, a convert to Islam may be different from someone who is a Muslim from birth. Conversion may be the expression of an important switch on a Galton machine leading to the rare event of being a perpetrator. The mass murder that occurred in the Norwegian town of Kongsberg in 2021 (Cotovio, Frater, & Kolirin, 2021) was enacted by a Danish citizen reported to have converted to Islam shortly before the attack (EFE, 2021). The personal issues of this individual may have been known in advance, and if so the act of conversion – given the known personal issues – could have been used as a warning signal.

Summarizing what has been explained so far, we have learned that searching for a needle in a haystack cannot be trivially reduced to anomaly detection. Moreover, needles are rare, and their etiology can reasonably be modeled through the Galton board, which helps us to see that this etiology involves unique and less probable paths in a phase space. Whenever we seek to find a needle in a haystack, we should spend some time with our simple Galton machine in order to represent the phase space of our system and to better identify the switches that may lead to the formation of our human needle. While there is no modeling protocol for such a process, it may be used as a thought experiment for the identification of weak signals indicating the approaching needle, and to help us build and simulate our models before using them in practice. Being a needle is the outcome of a complex process and not the process itself. Identifying the "wind coming from the sea" (see Chapter 2) may therefore be highly important for understanding the tattered curtains.

REFERENCES

Boyden, L. M., Mao, J., Belsky, J., Mitzner, L., Farhi, A., Mitnick, M. A., … & Lifton, R. P.. (2002). High bone density due to a mutation in LDL-receptor–related protein 5. *New England Journal of Medicine*, 346, 1513–1521. doi:10.1056/NEJMoa013444

Cotovio, V., Frater, J., & Kolirin, L. (2021, October 14). Suspect charged after 5 killed in bow and arrow attack in Norway, police say. CNN. Retrieved January 19, 2022, from https://edition.cnn.com/2021/10/13/europe/kongsberg-norway-attack-intl/index.html

EFE. (2021, October 14). Norway police: Bow and arrow attacker is Muslim convert known to authorities. Retrieved January 19, 2022, from https://www.efe.com/efe/english/portada/norway-police-bow-and-arrow-attacker-is-muslim-convert-known-to-authorities/50000260-4651656

National Weather Service. (n.d.). How dangerous is lightning? Weather.gov. Retrieved January 19, 2022, from https://www.weather.gov/safety/lightning-odds

Sepulveda, I. (2021, May 2). Odds of 50 random events happening to you. Stacker. Retrieved January 19, 2022, from https://stacker.com/stories/2343/odds-50-random-events-happening-you

Wikipedia. (2022a). Principle of indifference. Retrieved January 19, 2022, from https://en.wikipedia.org/wiki/Principle_of_indifference

Wikipedia. (2022b). Probability distribution. Retrieved January 19, 2022, from https://en.wikipedia.org/wiki/Probability_distribution.

Crying Wolf

4

False Alarms and Their Price

For some interesting cultural reasons, psychopaths are disproportionally represented in cinema and TV series. From *Dexter* (2006–2013) to *The Joker* (2019), these disturbed figures are presented as heroes, gain interest, and unfortunately acquire some form of admiration, with some people even identifying with them. From a psychological perspective, the antisocial psychopathic personality has three main traits: manipulativeness; impulsiveness, sometimes associated with thrill-seeking; and a lack of empathy and remorse (Westen, Shedler, Bradley, & DeFife, 2012). In several context, identifying or diagnosing psychopaths may be highly important. For instance, some sensitive positions require rational individuals whom we can fully trust and who have clear moral norms preventing them from crossing certain lines, even when they face strong temptations, whether financial, sexual, or another type. A Central Intelligence Agency (CIA) case officer who crosses a line by collaborating with Afghan drug dealers may be motivated by pure greed. As a result, they may also have been exposed to blackmail by a foreign intelligence agency and might also become an insider threat. Those two forms of unacceptable behavior must be prevented in advance by carefully screening potential candidates for the position, including by screening for a psychopathic signature. Although a degree of psychopathy (i.e. soft psychopathy) may even be required for certain operative positions, there is a line separating "soft" and "functional" psychopaths from their pathological counterparts. For example, *XXX* (2002) is an action film featuring Vin Diesel as the hero (Xander Cage), who is a thrill seeker recruited by the National Security Agency (NSA) for a special mission. To enter a Russian terrorist group, our hero must be manipulative enough to convince the group's leader that he can be trusted. Our special agent, XXX, is clearly a charming manipulator. Additionally, to be sent on such a dangerous mission, our hero must be a thrill seeker, which he is. And, to create the necessary affiliation with the anarchistic terrorist group, he must also be rebellious, which he definitely is, as can be seen from the opening scene of the movie.

Cage is characterized by clear psychopathic dimensions but on the relatively soft and functional range of the spectrum. He feels empathy for human beings and has his own moral standards. Sending a Mormon on a mission to enter a Russian terrorist organization would probably result in failure, as would sending people from such a background as CIA officers to Afghanistan (Laux & Pezzullo, 2016). For missions of this kind, the Cage type seems to be the most appropriate rather than a devoted Mormon who graduated in finance from the University of Utah. The imprecise boundary between a functional personality and a dangerous one serves as an example to illustrate the difficulty of identifying a needle in a haystack. Soft psychopaths are more difficult to distinguish from pathological psychopaths than pathological psychopaths from "normal" human beings. However, this is exactly the place where the "edge" is (see Chapter 2).

Antisocial psychopathic personality *disorder* signals the extreme and dysfunctional end of the spectrum. It is a rare disorder, with estimates suggesting that it characterizes 1% or less of the population (e.g. Holzer et al., 2020; Sanz-García, Gesteira, Sanz, & García-Vera, 2021; Werner, Few, & Bucholz, 2015). Although we may think about psychopaths in binary terms, following the psychodynamic approach in psychology (Lingiardi & McWilliams, 2017), the antisocial psychopathic personality may be considered to be located on a spectrum ranging from highly empathic and considerate people to non-empathic, manipulative, and exploitive individuals. To understand the idea that personalities can range over a spectrum, let's recall a prominent Jewish sage who is identified with the idea of empathy.

Hillel the Elder, who was born in Babylon 110 BCE, is known for an ethical imperative that I personally like: "That which is hateful to you, do not do to your fellow. That is the whole Torah; the rest is the explanation; go and learn" (Babylonian Talmud, Shabat 31a). Hillel emphasized the fact that the whole of the Torah – or the teachings given to the Jewish people (and all other human beings) – can be reduced, if necessary, to a single teaching: do not do to others what you as a human being don't like others to do to you, because others probably feel the same as you. This is a simple lesson in empathy that it is not trivial to apply, as the idea of a "fellow" extends to all human beings. For most people, empathy is contextualized; they may feel empathy for their own children while giving no mercy to the children of their enemies or even to the children of other people geographically and ethnically remote from them. The UN (n.d.) reports that 350,209 individuals were killed under Bashar al-Assad's regime in Syria, including 27,126 children. Let me repeat this horrible number: 27,126 children were killed as a result of Assad's struggle to retain absolute power. Surprisingly, some progressive politicians in the

USA, such as a specific congresswoman, are not promoting any boycott on Assad's regime of terror or on any of his allies directly involved in the mass murder of citizens. You will not hear them arguing to boycott caviar from Russia or pistachios from Iran, the two main supporters of Assad's regime. The explanations or justifications for this specific moral and political preference are less important than the outcome, which is a clear expression of *contextual empathy*. As you can see, empathy is contextualized, which means that the line differentiating psychopaths from non-psychopaths is not as clear as might be imagined. Hillel the Elder calls for a different moral approach to empathy, one that is more universal. If subjected to our psychopathy test, Hillel would probably have been located at the lowest end of the distribution, together with people such as the educator and Holocaust victim Janusz Korczak. In contrast, individuals such as Ted Bundy, Charles Manson, Adolf Hitler, and too many other people would probably have been located at the highest end of the distribution.

Let's imagine that the scores on a psychopathy test will normally distribute (see Chapter 3), with a mean of 60 and a standard deviation of 10. Let's say that the majority of people (i.e. around 68%) are located between scores 50 and 70. Finally, let's assume that I am tested and my psychopathy score is 81. Wow! This is high. Now, the question is whether it is more likely that I am a psychopath or a non-psychopath. Most of the students to whom I have presented this question over the years have concluded that a score of 81 – two standard deviations above the mean – is strong evidence for diagnosing their professor as a psychopath. On the individual level of analysis, they may or may not be wrong. However, think about a population of 100,000 individuals, all of whom have taken our test and now make up our distribution of psychopathy scores. Out of the whole population, 1,000 individuals (i.e. 1%) are expected to be psychopaths. In the normal distribution, the range encompassing two standard deviations above the mean accounts for 95.5%[1] of our population. This leaves us with 4.5% of the population scoring above 80. Now, even if all of the 1,000 psychopaths scored 81 or above, this leaves us with 3,550 (i.e. 4,550 − 1,000) individuals who are not psychopaths. This means that even if I scored 81 or higher, the odds (i.e. the ratio between the probability of being a non-psychopath and the probability of being a psychopath) of me being a non-psychopath would be 3.7 (i.e. 0.78 ÷ 0.21), meaning almost four times higher than the odds of me being a psychopath. Consequently, if you want to bet whether your professor is a psychopath or not and you are basing your bet on their score alone, then the most rational bet is against the hypothesis that they are a psychopath, even if your grade from their course leads you to think differently.

Therefore, the difficulty of distinguishing between the needle and the stalks of hay may be expressed by the number of *false positives* (FPs) – that is, cases where the stalks of hay are falsely reported to be needles. This is a tricky problem that has been insightfully explained by Wainer and Savage (2008), and it surprisingly appears even if we use a powerful diagnostic test for needles. Let me briefly explain this idea, which I will further develop later, in order to clarify why is it difficult to distinguish the needle from the haystack. For this explanation, I will use a variation on Wainer and Savage's original example.

Let's return to Edward Snowden, who we first encountered in Chapter 1. Let's imagine that his former colleagues at the NSA are still living under the trauma of September 11, 2001, and the moral implicative of "Never Again." Using their powerful surveillance technologies, they seek to identify potential terrorists by analyzing the metadata of internet users. As the terrorist attacks of right-wing white supremacists (e.g. in the Oklahoma City bombing of 1995) are no less worrying than potential attacks by radical Islamists, they may cover both threats. For brevity, we will use the radical Islamic threat only.

Snowden's former colleagues are specifically interested in those people who visit websites relating to radical Islam. The hypothetical population under surveillance includes 300 million people. The number of actual terrorists is estimated to be 3,000 people, or only 0.00001% of the population. We may further assume that in order to honor their former colleague, the NSA has developed a powerful threat identification system called Edy.

Before I present Edy, let me explain the difference between screening and diagnosis. In contrast with diagnosis, where the aim is to confirm or rule out the hypothesis that a *specific individual* has a certain attribute, screening is broadly used to determine which member of a large group of individuals has the attribute in question (Steiner, 2003). In the real world, these processes must be practically combined, as first a large group of individuals is screened and then an in-depth diagnosis (or inspection) is applied. Here we start with screening.

Edy boasts 99% accuracy in identifying terrorists. This means that by using the metadata of individuals under surveillance, Edy can successfully identify 99% of the terrorists. The performance of a diagnostic system, such as Edy, is usually presented using a confusion matrix. Table 4.1 shows the general form of a confusion matrix.

TABLE 4.1   The general form of a confusion matrix

TEST	OBSERVATION	
	POSITIVE	NEGATIVE
Positive	True positives (hits)	False positives (false alarms)
Negative	False negatives (misses)	True negatives (correct rejections)

The test or the system decides which case belongs to which category of positive versus negative cases. For instance, Edy may be asked to decide whether an individual is a terrorist (i.e. positive) or not. The test's decision is then checked against the real label or the actual observation. The test may decide that an instance is positive. If this decision is confirmed, the cases will appear in the upper left cell of the matrix among what we call true positives (i.e. TPs) or "hits." In contrast, the test may err, and if so we will observe FPs or "false alarms" because the test has mistakenly tagged a case as positive when it was actually negative. Alternatively, the test may decide that the examined case does not show the sign of the thing we are looking for and will therefore tag the case as negative. If the test is correct, then the case is a true negative (TN) or "correct rejection"; however, if the test "misses" the case, then we describe its erroneous decision as a "false negative" (FN).

By organizing the true data against the test's decisions, we may evaluate its performance using various measures. For example, *sensitivity* (i.e. the TP rate) is the proportion of cases that receive a positive result on the test out of those that actually have the "condition." It is described in machine learning (ML) as "recall" and actually describes the ratio of "targets" we are able to identify out of all targets. *Specificity*, also described as the "TN rate," refers to the proportion of cases that receive a negative result on the test out of those that do not actually have the condition. This is the recall rate of those that are non-targets. Sensitivity and specificity are two important diagnostic measures in medicine as they involve the idea of ruling in or ruling out (Lee, 1999). A highly sensitive test means that it performs well in detecting individuals with a disease. It is like a fishing net capable of catching even the smallest fish. A highly specific test, on the other hand, restricts the number of subjects without the disease who have a positive result on the test. This simply means that the ideal test or system is one that recognizes all targets while having no false alarms. In ML, the performance measure of *accuracy* assesses the correctness of the test's decisions.

It must be noted that in some real-world situations, the price of FPs is such that we would not be willing to compromise on the sensitivity of the test. For example, the price of a traitor within an organization may be such that we would like to identify all suspicious individuals despite the possibility of false alarms. Prices are contextual. When candidates are selected for positions in the intelligence community, employers work according to the principle of "if there is doubt, there is no doubt." This may result in a potentially talented case officer being ruled out by the selection procedure, but this is a legitimate price to pay to avoid the risk of hiring someone who could harm the system if they were allowed to enter the organization.

Let us return to Edy and its diagnostic performance. Tables 4.1A and 4.1B present the diagnostic performance of Edy. The system (i.e. the test) provides

TABLE 4.1A   The performance of Edy

TEST (EDY)	OBSERVATION	
	TERRORIST	NON-TERRORIST
Positive	2,970 (99%)	
Negative		
	N = 3,000	

TABLE 4.1B   The performance of Edy in numbers

TEST (EDY)	OBSERVATION	
	TERRORIST	NON-TERRORIST
Positive	2,970 (hit)	2,999,970 (false positive)
Negative	30 (miss)	296,997,030 (correct rejection)
Sum	3,000	299,997,000

us with a binary signal, which is "positive" or "negative." As in medical diagnosis, a positive signal has a negative meaning. In our context, a positive signal may indicate that the individual is a terrorist. Such a binary decision made by the system may be the result of integrating several features to produce a score that crosses a certain threshold. For example, imagine a young Muslim male who is an enthusiastic reader of *Dabiq*, a former magazine of ISIS. Edy considers this behavior to be a warning signal. Edy also notes that after the man's favorite magazine is blocked, he starts to use the anonymizing software Tor, raising the suspicion that he is following the advice of Edward Snowden to escape surveillance. These two signals may mark the young man as a potential terrorist.

As introduced above, the performance of systems like Edy is commonly measured by comparing the system's decision with the real observation (i.e. whether those marked as positive or negative are really terrorists or non-terrorists). The system correctly identifies 99% of the terrorists, meaning that out of 3,000 terrorists, Edy successfully identifies 2,970 individuals, whose names are then delivered to the local Federal Bureau of Investigation (FBI) offices for in-depth inspection. Of the 299,997,000 non-terrorists, only 1% will be falsely reported as terrorists. Sounds good, doesn't it? However, when we translate this percentage into numbers, we find that 2,999,970 individuals will be falsely reported as terrorists. The ratio between falsely and truly identified terrorist is 1,000:1!

What does this mean in our attempt to understand the difficulty of distinguishing the needle from the stalks of hay? It means that even with an almost perfect diagnostic system (reaching 99% "accuracy"), most targeted needles will be innocent stalks of hay. Moreover, there will be prices accompanying this level of error: too many objects will be marked for in-depth inspection, which will overload the local FBI offices; some of the stalks of hay may become terrorists as a result of being unfairly tagged as such; and so on. Trying to identify rare objects within the limits of a diagnostic test inevitably invites a high level of FPs – hence my initial observation that the needle is difficult to distinguish from the haystack. This difficulty of recognition is painfully expressed by the price of FPs. To better explain the price of FPs, let me take you to a totally different field: industrial production.

THE PRICE OF FALSE ALARMS

The pulp-and-paper industry involves companies using wood to produce paper. A paper machine is used for the mass production of paper, and, like any other machine, these machines sometimes get stuck. To illustrate this point, let us use data (Ranjan, Reddy, Mustonen, Paynabar, & Pourak, 2018) taken from a paper manufacturing machine, where paper breakage is a rare but highly costly event. The prevalence of paper breakage is low: only 124 cases out of 18,398 records, which as a rounded percentage is less than 1% (0.7%). However, the cost of breakage is high. A failure entails that production must be stopped, at a cost of $10,000 per hour (C. Ranjan, ProcessMiner/Atlanta, GA, personal communication, 2021). Over the period covered by the dataset (around a month), the loss caused by the machine failures was $1.24 million. In one of my papers (Neuman, Cohen, & Erez, 2021), my colleagues and I attempted to predict an approaching failure using a dataset that included predictor variables ($x_1–x_{61}$) gathered from the sensors of the machine.

Let us assume that checking and verifying that there is no problem consumes 10 minutes of work at a cost of $1,667 (i.e. [$10,000/60_{min}$] × 10 min). What we can see is that the cost of a false alarm is such that it must be taken into account when we propose a solution that would send an alarm saying that a problem is coming and that the machine must be stopped and checked. The benefits of any predictive or classification system should be estimated against the price of false alarms or FPs.

As argued by Savage (2012), it is not uncertainty per se that we wish to resolve but the risk accompanying it. As risk involves cost and is "in the eye of the beholder" (Savage, 2012, p. 154), Savage proposes adopting a "risk attitude" rather than an unrealistic form of utility theory and a decontextualized attitude where uncertainly is measured in a purely academic context regardless of real-world costs and benefits. My colleagues and I followed Savage in describing the costs accompanying the use of various ML classifiers to predict an approaching failure in the production machine. First, we used the 60 continuous features (i.e. measurements of sensors) in the dataset. For each continuous variable, we defined three measures of change. In other words, we defined three measures of change for each sensor's measurement. The first measure was:

$$\delta_{xi\_ratio} = \frac{xi\_t}{xi_{t-1}}$$

This is simply the ratio between the sensor's value at a given minute and the value at the previous minute. The second measure is the average ratio of change between a measurement and its previous measurement, and between the previous measurement and the one preceding it:

$$\delta_{xi\_ratio\_2} = \frac{1}{2}\left(\frac{xi\_t}{xi\_{t-1}} + \frac{xi\_{t-1}}{xi\_{t-2}}\right)$$

The third measure is the ratio between the previous two measurements:

$$\delta_{xi\_ratio\_ratio} = \frac{\delta_{xi\_ratio}}{\delta_{xi\_ratio\_2}}$$

Following Savage (2012), we cannot use the classifiers' performance measures per se but must evaluate them in the practical context of risk and decision-making. In this case, the FP is a crucial measure. Given the cost saved through a TP (i.e. hit or identifying the failure in advance), which is $10,000 per hour, the cost of missing a failure (i.e. FN), which is the same, and the estimated cost of a false alarm (i.e. FP), which we assume to minimally be 5 minutes of work (approximately $833), we can easily compute the benefit of a classifier through the following equation:

$$\text{MONEY SAVED} = TP \times \text{Cost}_{TP} - FP \times \text{Cost}_{FP}$$

or, in terms of hours of work saved (HWS):

$$HWS = TP - FN \div 12$$

where an hour of work is priced at $10,000.

To illustrate the importance of the above two measures (i.e. HWS and MONEY SAVED), consider the following analysis that my colleagues and I performed. Here comes a highly technical section and the reader who has no interest in it, may simply skip it. As the dataset was imbalanced, with less than 1% of the cases characterized as defects in the machine, we used an ML classifier with a weighted training procedure and scaling of the features. When using the Linear SVM classifier, we gained 60% recall and 0.6% precision, meaning that we would have been able to identify 60% of the problems in advance but with a price. Given a TP of $N = 75$, we would have correctly anticipated a failure and stopped the machine 75 times at a cost of $750,000 instead of $1,240,000. This is clearly a significant saving in production costs. However, and here is the problem, this classifier produced $N = 12,801$ cases of FPs, where production would have needed to be stopped and the machine checked despite the fact that *no real problem existed*. Even if we assume that it takes only 1 minute of work to verify that an FP is not a real failure in production, then the cost of the FPs (i.e. $2,124,966) accompanying our "successful" classifier would be such as to make the use of the classifier irrelevant for all practical purposes. Here we can see that the benefits of using a successful classifier – which may save a lot of money by identifying failures in advance – are reversed when the price of false alarms is taken into account.

The use of ML to detect extremely rare events may be accompanied by several problems that cannot be addressed even by the weighted training methodology that we applied to handle the imbalanced dataset. First, the cross-validation method may be biased concerning imbalanced sets (He & Ma, 2013) because the distribution of cases is skewed and might distort the representation of the minority class in the folds. The way to address this difficulty is to apply *stratified k-fold cross-validation*. Therefore, we reanalyzed the data using a stratified 10-fold cross-validation procedure with weighted training and scaling of the features. Some classifiers (such as Decision Tree, Linear SVM, and GaussianNB) failed to produce any significant results, showing how sensitive an ML model is to various specifications. The results of the top three classifiers are presented in Table 4.2.

TABLE 4.2   Performance of the three best classifiers

CLASSIFIER	RECALL (%)	PRECISION (%)	HOURS OF WORK SAVED (HWS)
Gradient Boosting	55	19	44
AdaBoost	57	15	39
Random Forest	64	12	29

Note: The baseline for comparison is 124 cases of machine failure with an accompanying cost of $1,240,000.

Let us examine the performance of the first classifier (Gradient Boosting). It produced 68 TPs, which means that using the classifier would enable us to predict 68 cases of failure in advance. Therefore, instead of working for 124 hours to correct undetectable failures, we could work for only 56 hours (with the remaining 56 hours resulting from our inability to correctly identify 56 of the failures in advance). We would therefore theoretically spend only $680,000 for the 68 working hours of fixing the machine instead of $1,240,000. However, this classifier also produced 286 FPs. This means that we have 286 cases of false alarms where we would need to stop the machine despite the fact that there is nothing wrong with it. If we assume that the minimum time for verifying a false alarm is 5 minutes, then, given the cost of an hour of work, working for 5 minutes should cost $833 (rounded) and the cost of 286 false alarms would be $238,238. Therefore, $441,762 (i.e. $680,000 − $238,238) is the actual amount of money we could save by applying the classifier. This sum is equal to 44 working hours (rounded) saved on fixing the machine. As you can see, even in the case of simple industrial production, the price of FPs must be considered when we propose a powerful diagnostic system. This case illustrates the price of FPs and their importance in any project seeking to address the needle challenge. In fact, the logic underlying this approach is equivalent to a motivation of the legendary investor Warren Buffett. As he wisely proposed in 1989 (cited in Griffin, 2015):

> Take the probability of loss times the amount of possible loss from the probability of gain times the amount of possible gain. That is what we're trying to do. It's imperfect, but that's what it's all about.

This advice is actually the classical idea of expected value analysis:

$$EV = \sum P(X_i) * X_i$$

where X_i is once the positive value of TPs and once the negative value of FNs. Surprisingly, data scientists are not always familiar with the importance of expected value analysis. An intelligent and highly experienced engineer once told me with pride that he had developed an algorithm for predicting increases in the price of stocks and making some money out of it. His enthusiasm was somehow diminished when I asked him about the prices of false alarms and false predictions. The overall lesson that we should learn is that FPs create a headache for the needle challenge. Without taking them into account, while using any data science methodology within the broader context of prices, we may gain excellent results with our ML algorithms; however, these will be results that have no true practical value. In the next chapter, I delve deeper into the reasons for the difficulties associated with the needle challenge.

NOTE

1. I round the numbers in many examples for ease of comprehension.

REFERENCES

Griffin, T. J. (2015). *Charlie Munger: The complete investor.* New York, NY: Columbia University Press.

He, H., & Ma, Y. (Eds.). (2013). *Imbalanced learning: Foundations, algorithms, and applications.* Piscataway, NJ: IEEE Press.

Holzer, K. J., Vaughn, M. G., Loux, T. M., Mancini, M. A., Fearn, N. E., & Wallace, C. L. (2020). Prevalence and correlates of antisocial personality disorder in older adults. *Aging & Mental Health, 26*, 1–10.

Laux, D., & Pezzullo, R. (2016). *Left of boom.* New York, NY: St. Martin's Press.

Lee, W. C. (1999). Selecting diagnostic tests for ruling out or ruling in disease: The use of the Kullback–Leibler distance. *International Journal of Epidemiology, 28*(3), 521–525.

Lingiardi, V., & McWilliams, N. (Eds.). (2017). *Psychodynamic diagnostic manual: PDM-2.* New York, NY: Guilford Press.

Neuman, Y., Cohen, Y., & Erez, E. (2021). Extreme rare events identification through Jaynes inferential approach. *Big Data, 9*(6). doi:10.1089/big.2021.0191

Ranjan, C., Reddy, M., Mustonen, M., Paynabar, K., & Pourak, K. (2018). *Dataset: Rare event classification in multivariate time series. arXiv preprint arXiv:1809.10717.*

Sanz-García, A., Gesteira, C., Sanz, J., & García-Vera, M. P. (2021). Prevalence of psychopathy in the general adult population: A systematic review and meta-analysis. *Frontiers in Psychology, 12*, 3278.

Savage, S. (2012). *The flaw of averages.* Hoboken, NJ: John Wiley & Sons.

Steiner, D. L. (2003). Diagnosing tests: Using and misusing diagnostic and screening tests. *Journal of Personality Assessment, 81*(3), 209–219.

UN. (n.d.). *Oral update on the extent of conflict-related deaths in the Syrian Arab Republic.* OHCHR. Retrieved January 19, 2022, from https://www.ohchr.org/EN/NewsEvents/Pages/DisplayNews.aspx?NewsID=27531&LangID=E

Wainer, H., & Savage, S. (2008). Visual revelations: Until proven guilty – False positives and the war on terror. *Chance, 21*(1), 55–58.

Werner, K. B., Few, L. R., & Bucholz, K. K. (2015). Epidemiology, comorbidity, and behavioral genetics of antisocial personality disorder and psychopathy. *Psychiatric Annals, 45*(4), 195–199.

Westen, D., Shedler, J., Bradley, B., & DeFife, J. A. (2012). An empirically derived taxonomy for personality diagnosis: Bridging science and practice in conceptualizing personality. *American Journal of Psychiatry, 169*(3), 273–284.

Why Is It Difficult to Find the Needle?

5

On Rare and Common Paths

The idea of false positives – discussed in the previous chapter – takes us back to the Galton machine (see Chapter 3). Take a look at Figure 5.1. You can see several paths, originating from the first peg at the top. These paths lead to the bins at the bottom. There is only one path leading from the top peg to the leftmost bin. You can see that the path leading to the leftmost bin involves left moves (i.e. L) only. The tree formed by the paths is symmetric and therefore the same observation holds for the rightmost bin, to which only one path leads. The leftmost path can be symbolized by the paths of left and right moves that lead to it: LLLLL. It is a path that involves left moves only and therefore it is homogenous. The same is true for the rightmost bin: RRRRR. This is a path that involves right moves only. How many paths lead to bins two and five from the left? The answer is five paths. For bin two from the left, these are the paths:

LLLLR
LLLRL
LLRLL
LRLLL
RLLLL

DOI: 10.1201/9781003289647-5

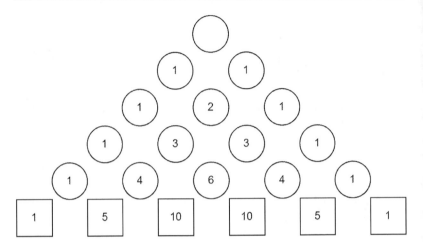

FIGURE 5.1   Paths on the Galton machine.

Source: Author.

As you can see, these paths differ from the leftmost path by a *single* letter (or move) only. Let's assume that the leftmost bin represents the rare event of being a psychopath. The difference between a pathological psychopath and a successfully functioning psychopath, represented by the second bin from the left, may be attributed to a single switch only, such as "impulsivity," or to a single feature or switch, such as a functioning family (see Chapter 3 for an introduction to the idea of switches). There may be only a single factor or switch differentiating between the pathological and the normal. The above paths leading to the more normative and prevalent bins may symbolize paths to "normality," which are slightly different from the paths to the anomaly of the leftmost bin. How many paths lead to the bin that is three from the left? There are 10 paths:

LLLRR
LRLRL
LRRLL
RLLRL
RLRLL
RRLLL
and so on

What we can see is a way of modeling how variability (or variety) is depicted through the Galton machine. Variability is the expression of complexity and, in our context, it results from the depth of the Galton machine. In Figure 5.1, the "normal" bins differ from our "needle" (i.e. the rare bin) by two letters only. The entropy of the most "normal" bin is the highest, while the outliers (i.e. the leftmost and rightmost bins) have the lowest entropy possible. This means that there are far more ways of being normal than ways of being non-normal. This observation is deeply connected with the Anna Karenina principle, which suggests that rare events or objects require far more conditions than non-rare ones in order to happen. For example, being a pathological psychopath may involve having some kind of genetic predisposition, a pathological family, and life experiences that lead to hopelessness, a lack of significant others, and so on. Only when all of these conditions are met does the antisocial psychopathic character – in its full manifestation – appear in front of our eyes. In contrast, in order to acquire merely a normally moderate neurotic personality, only one condition may be sufficient.

Normal objects, classes, or bins express the *maximum heterogeneity of paths leading to them*, and the Galton machine – through its simple structure and full ignorance – shows how the more common outcomes are characterized by the maximum variety of paths. I have found this to be an interesting observation, for several reasons. First, the variety of the "non-needles," as formed by the Galton machine, is such that the features of normal cases overlap with those of the outliers. This explains why it is difficult to distinguish between the needle and the haystack and why the problem of false positives *inevitably* appears when we try to address the needle challenge. The Galton machine produces outcomes that are not sharply demarcated from the outliers but "normal" outcomes that overlap with the rarest outcomes. The path leading to the rarest bin only slightly differs from the path leading to its neighboring bin. Using the Galton machine, we may understand rare objects not as qualitatively different; instead, the difference is of a quantitative nature. Second, paradoxically, the most interesting outcomes are the normal ones as they have more heterogenous paths leading to them. There are more ways of being normal than being deviant, an observation that calls into question the romantic approach to deviation propagated in the past (through the false association between madness and creativity) or celebrated today in the mass media and entertainment industry (which like to show us "interesting" characters). In contrast with what we may be falsely led to believe, normal families are much more interesting than deviant families, and the life of a common human being is much more interesting, at least from a certain perspective, than the life of a shallow fictitious character such as the psychopath Hannibal Lecter from *The Silence of the Lambs* (1991). The entropy of the paths leading to the rare outcomes is lower, but it must be clarified that this observation does not tell us about the magnitude of variation *within* the normal and the pathological groups. It tells us only about the etiology of the formation of a rare event, which is much more distinct and simpler than the etiology of the formation of a normal individual.

One of the difficulties in recognizing a needle is that the measured features of the members of the rare class may express a great range of values. For example, if we measure a binary feature such as a disturbed childhood (0 or 1), then we may learn that the few cases of insiders that we are familiar with present a spectrum of values; while Chelsea Manning (born Bradley Edward Manning) is reported to have had a disturbed childhood (Wikipedia, 2022), Edward Snowden is not. The range of values characterizing the very small sample of needles available to us is such that these values cannot be used to test the hypothesis that a person belongs to the needle class by simply comparing insiders to non-insiders. Thus, the range of values characterizing the features of the sample of needles is very high, but this observation does not seem to go hand in hand with the above observation that there are fewer paths leading to the rare bins or outcomes. However, one possible explanation for this range of values is simple. Although there are fewer paths leading to the rare objects, the variance we observe in the smaller sample of deviant members of a certain outcome (e.g. psychopaths) is greater than the variance of *features* among the members of the normal majority group, because *by definition* the variance (or the standard deviation) – which is a statistical measure of disparity around the mean – is a function of the sample's size:

$$s = \sqrt{\frac{\sum_{i=1}^{n} (x_i - \bar{x})^2}{n}}$$

where we first measure each observation's (x_i) difference from the sample's mean ($\bar{x}$) and then raise this difference to the power of two, summing all of these outcomes, dividing them by the sample's size (n), and extracting the root of this expression. Observing a larger variability of a feature, among members of a small sample of rare objects, is therefore a trivial result of using the sample size for the measurement. In other words, the greater variability of features measured among members of the minority group (i.e. the sample of needles) is a trivial derivative of the sample's size. Given this variability, it is difficult to use a set of features to discriminate between a needle and the rest of the haystack. One less trivial implication of this potentially higher variance among the members of the deviant group is that it may be *strategically* used by the needles for camouflage. This point will be discussed in Chapter 8.

As we are using the concept of information, let us think about the needle challenge in terms of *Shannon information entropy*. Shannon entropy is a measure of information defined in terms of surprise and probabilities. Imagine a perfectly balanced coin that, over the long run, shows heads in 50% of the cases and tails in the rest. The probabilities of observing the different outcomes (i.e. heads or tails) are equal (i.e. $p = 0.5$). Now, when I toss a coin and show you the outcome, your surprise will be full as you will not have had any reasonable grounds to prefer one outcome over the other. Your full ignorance will have led you to no preferences for this outcome or the other and therefore whatever the outcome of the toss is, you will be fully surprised. You will be fully surprised because you could not have expected the outcome. This is a situation where the surprise is maximal, and this surprise is expressed by the Shannon information measure, which proposes that information is the function of our prior preferences or expectations.

So, to return to the discussion in the previous chapter, what is the entropy associated with screening for terrorists through Edy? In the case of the terrorists, we have two possible outcomes: terrorist and non-terrorist. However, in this case and given the low prevalence of terrorists, we have almost perfect certainty that an individual randomly picked out from the population will be a non-terrorist. In this case, the Shannon entropy is calculated as follows:

$$H(X) = \sum p(x_i) \log \frac{1}{p(x_i)}$$

The answer approaches 0. This means that we are almost certain that an individual randomly picked out of the haystack will be a non-terrorist. This is our rational working assumption. Now, let's improve our situation by bringing Edy into the picture. Edy provides us with a signal about whether someone is a terrorist, and this signal may be used in a decision tree classification model as shown in Figure 5.2.

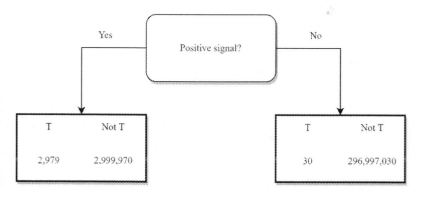

FIGURE 5.2 A decision model for identifying a terrorist.

Source: Author.

How informative is the signal provided by Edy? How informative is the split it produces? Given the probabilities of someone being a terrorist ($p = 0.00001$) or a non-terrorist ($p = 0.99999$), the original entropy of our dataset (H) is almost zero (i.e. 0.0001). The entropy of the split is therefore:

$$0.01 \times 0.001 + 0.99 \times 0.001 = 0.001$$

where 0.01 is the relative size of the individuals identified by Edy as terrorists and 0.99 is the relative size of the set identified by Edy as non-terrorists. The uncertainty has changed from 0.0001 to 0.001 and the *information gain*, or the amount of entropy that we have removed, is:

Information Gain $= 0.001 - 0.0001 = 0.0009$

This means that despite the high accuracy of the system, our uncertainty (which was very low from the beginning) is still close to zero.

Shannon entropy does not fully represent the uncertainty of our imbalanced dataset, and there are alternative ways of representing our uncertainty. These lessons may direct us to use a different measure of uncertainty, such as Tsallis entropy:

$$S_q(p_i) = \frac{1}{q-1}\left(1 - \sum p_i^q\right)$$

where the q index is used to emphasize the probability of rare events when it is lower than 1 or give more weight to common events when it is higher than 1. Let's compute the uncertainty of our dataset, this time using Tsallis entropy and $q = 0.8$. If we operate this form of entropy calculation with a super-additive index that amplifies the probability of being a terrorist, our entropy score becomes 0.075 – much higher than the degree of uncertainty produced by the Shannon measure. Using an entropy index of 0.01, the entropy becomes 0.94. This means that by weighting the different probabilities of the outcomes, we can see that our certainty may be lower than what was proposed to us by the previous measure. As argued by Wilk and Włodarczyk (2008, p. 4809), "the way in which one collects information about an object decides the form of the corresponding information entropy." In contrast with some naïve assumptions, the kinds of questions we ask invite the kinds of answers we get, and the form of information entropy we use should be adapted to the specific question we ask. The Shannon information measure can be interpreted in terms of the number of binary questions we need to ask in order to locate an object. Here is an example that I use to explain this idea to my students.

One of our cats, named Kitmon, likes to nap in hidden places. Let's imagine that there are eight drawers (i.e. cells) where the cat may peacefully nap. Having no prior information about the cat's preferred location, we face complete uncertainty and therefore must assign equal probabilities to each cell: $p = 0.125$. We now start searching for the cat by asking a series of binary questions. Assuming the drawers are vertically organized, the first question is whether the cat is napping in the top four drawers. Given either a positive or a negative answer, we can reduce our problem space by half. If we gain a positive answer, we now know that the cat is napping in one of the top four drawers, so our next question is whether he is napping in the top two drawers. Once this has been answered, we are left with two drawers only and have to ask one last question before we can find out where the lazy creature is napping. The maximum number of binary questions is therefore three. The average number of questions (or tree splits) that we have to ask ourselves to find a terrorist in the abovementioned dataset by using Shannon information entropy is less than one. However, when we use the version based on Tsallis entropy, we realize that the number of questions required to identify a terrorist may be much higher as a simple function of the emphasis we give to the less probable outcome of being a terrorist.

In Chapter 7, I explain why identifying an object through binary questions is not as simple as we may imagine because there is a difference between localization and recognition. For now, I would like to sum up the discussion so far. To identify a needle in a haystack, the hit rate of Edy (i.e. TPs) is not enough, and the way we conceptualize our uncertainty has direct consequences for understanding the difficulty of finding the needle. As the rarity of the needle in the haystack is given and cannot be changed, it seems that our only hope may come from better understanding of the diagnostic process and the way we search for a needle in a haystack. However, given the above examples, it seems that we have some mental bugs in our understanding of the diagnostic process and how difficult it is to find a needle in a haystack. One of these possible bugs, together with a possible solution, is discussed in the next chapter.

REFERENCES

Wikipedia. (2022). Chelsea Manning. Retrieved March 30, 2022, from https://en.wikipedia.org/wiki/Chelsea_Manning.

Wilk, G., & Włodarczyk, Z. (2008). Example of a possible interpretation of Tsallis entropy. *Physica A: Statistical Mechanics and Its Applications, 387*(19–20), 4809–4813.

Why Do We Fail to Find the Needle?

6

The Binary Fallacy and the Bayesian Approach

The previous chapter explained that the difficulty of distinguishing the needle in the haystack is deeply associated with the problem of false positives (FPs). In this chapter, I would like to point to the more basic difficulty, which is that of getting a binary answer from screening or a diagnostic system. This mental "trap" or fallacy is the same as what is observed in traditional hypothesis testing, where a binary answer is provided in terms of statistical significance. The enormous difficulties associated with tests for statistical significance have been discussed since the 1960s (e.g. Bakan, 1966; Cohen, 1994), but a more bothersome issue is the persistence of the binary approach to hypothesis testing – a persistence probably grounded in our wishful thinking (i.e. our desire to gain simple and conclusive answers). Let me first explain the difficulty, and I will then introduce a constructive way to address it through the idea of Bayesian inference.

Bayesian inference is the process of updating our beliefs by considering some sort of evidence. For example, imagine a British thriller where a famous detective arrives at a castle to solve the mysterious murder of the owner. Ten people were at the castle during the murder and there is no evidence

DOI: 10.1201/9781003289647-6

whatsoever that the murderer was an outsider. Therefore, we have 10 suspects. As our detective initially has full ignorance, he assigns equal probabilities of being the murderer to each of the 10 suspects. The hypothesis that any one of the suspects is the murderer is therefore scored as 0.10. This number represents our detective's prior beliefs.

Before proceeding, a word or two should be said about how we should determine the prior, which is the initial degree of belief we assign to a given hypothesis. First, notice that the prior probability of guilt is a simple function of the population size. If you have 10 suspects, then the prior odds of any one of them being the murderer are 1 to 9 ($p = 0.11$). However, if we have a population of 1 million suspects then the prior odds are 0.000001. The larger the population, the smaller the prior probability of finding a needle and the smaller the weight of any evidence in changing the prior beliefs. Let's think about this interesting point, which is highly relevant to the needle challenge, using a biblical example.

The book of Exodus (32:4) tells us about the Sin of the Golden Calf, where, only a few months after gaining significant evidence for the existence of God through the miracle of crossing the Red Sea, the Israelites sinned by worshiping a golden idol. The evidence for the existence of God seemed to be impressive. After all, it was God who, through his miraculous intervention, had freed the Israelites from the tyranny of Pharaoh and led them through the Red Sea by splitting it. Whether you believe in this story or not is a minor issue. The really interesting issue is that in Bayesian terms, if the most powerful evidence for the existence of God did not convince the stubborn Israelites, then it says something about their *prior belief* in the existence of God. In other words, from the fact that the Israelites did not change their prior belief, given the strong weight of evidence to which they were exposed, we may infer that their prior belief in the existence of God was so low that even such an impressive miracle as splitting the Red Sea was largely ineffective in updating their belief. On the other hand, a different explanation is that the Israelites were impressively stubborn people who refused to change their belief not because their prior belief was so low but because they didn't let *any* evidence change their beliefs. This may be a nicely amusing explanation of why the Israelites are depicted as the chosen people in the Bible. If they accepted the existence of God, then these stubborn people would be the last to abandon their fate regardless of any challenging evidence.

In the context of the needle challenge, where the prior odds of identifying the needle are extremely low, it seems that even strong evidence might have a negligible influence on updating our prior beliefs, and this is a problem. In the context of the needle challenge, we may now understand that it is crucially important to *reduce the size of the haystack*. Reducing the size of the haystack is no less important than finding the evidence "incriminating" the specific needle. This approach of first reducing the size of the haystack is far from trivial and corresponds with up-to-date knowledge in neuroscience suggesting that attention is primarily about filtering out irrelevant information rather than picking relevant information only (Cepelewicz, 2019). The neuroscience perspective not only directs us to the importance of filtering out irrelevant information but also points to the fact that in natural cognitive systems, *recognition* is intertwined with *action*; we perceive and recognize in order to *act* in a certain way. When a chameleon recognizes a fly, it does not do it for the sake of recognition but with the practical aim of snapping out its tongue (i.e. a motor behavior) to catch the fly. Compare this naturalistic and deep association between recognition and action with the all-too-common approach in data science projects, where a gap commonly exists between those who analyze the data and those who make the decisions and take the actions. It is as if two separate brains exist for data analysis and decision-making, which from any ecological perspective is an unjustified anomaly. We can now understand that reducing the size of the haystack is highly justified both from the statistical Bayesian perspective and from the perspective of neuroscience. In the next chapter, this important shift in how to approach the needle challenge will be used to introduce the idea of "impostors' cues" and the way they may help us to address the challenge. Moreover, we will learn that attention and action should be seen as two facets of the same operating system. This point will be elaborated (also in the next chapter) in the context of what I would like to describe as *prioritization-based action*.

Establishing an acceptable prior probability is far from a trivial issue, especially in the context of criminal evidence. Some highly interesting suggestions have been proposed, including Fenton, Lagnado, Dahlman, and Neil's (2019) "opportunity prior," although this idea is less relevant to our needle challenge, as the needle challenge does not clearly involve a crime scene or the identification of the time of the crime.

Where we are sure about the prior, such as where we are sure that an individual is guilty or innocent, then there is no point in updating our beliefs. However, in between full confidence in one hypothesis or its complementary hypothesis, there is a gray area where the updating of beliefs can take place. In this gray zone of belief, establishing prior probability is a challenge. We may assume total ignorance and the maximum level of entropy. However, this is only one possible choice among others. In order to explain the Bayesian method of inference, we proceed with the simple idea of priors.

Assuming that our detective doesn't have a clear preference for one suspect or another, he will start collecting evidence in order to update his prior beliefs. For example, he may find a blood spot on the butler's collar, and forensic examination may prove this to be the blood of the victim. The probability that the butler did it, given this new piece of evidence, is now updated. How helpful is this evidence? The weight of evidence is formalized by the likelihood ratio (LR), also known as the Bayes factor (BF), which measures "the probative value of the evidence with respect to a specific hypothesis" (Fenton & Neil, 2021, p. 1):

$$BF = \frac{P(D|H)}{P(D|-H)}$$

The BF[1] should be read as follows: the ratio between the probability (P) of observing a piece of evidence or data (D) (e.g. blood spot belonging to the victim) given the hypothesis (H) (i.e. that X is the murderer) and the probability of observing the evidence given the alternative hypothesis that the person is not the murderer. If the probability of observing the evidence given the hypothesis is equal to the probability of observing the evidence given the alternative hypothesis, then the BF is 1, and the evidence has no value for updating our prior beliefs. In our case, if the BF is 1, then the blood spot found on the butler's collar has no value for updating the prior belief that he is the murderer and assigning to this hypothesis a higher probability. The BF is therefore a crucial feature in updating our prior beliefs. Let me further illustrate the importance of the BF, this time using Edy (originally introduced in Chapter 4).

Edy uses metadata, such as the D of visiting a radical Islamic website. How informative is this piece of evidence? To answer this question, we must calculate the probability of visiting a radical Islamic site *given* that our individual is a terrorist:

$$P(D/H) = ?$$

where D is probability of visiting a radical Islamic website and H is the probability of the individual being a terrorist.

To answer this question, we must perform a retrospective analysis of known terrorists and check how many of them visited radical Islamic websites before launching their attacks. Let's assume that we have the records of 100 terrorists, 90 of whom visited radical Islamic sites before launching their attack. The ratio of visiting a radical Islamic website *and* being a terrorist to the total number of terrorists is therefore 0.90, which sounds impressive. However, this number is meaningless without checking the probability of a person visiting a radical Islamic site without being a terrorist. In a population of 1 million non-terrorists, let's say that 10,000 have visited a radical Islamic site (1%). The BF is therefore 90 (i.e. 0.90 ÷ 0.01), which is a huge ratio by common standards. This number is indicative of the strength of the evidence we are using. Moreover, it is the factor by which we can transform our prior odds in support of the hypothesis that our individual is a terrorist:

$$H_t = \frac{P(H_t)}{P(-H_t)}$$

into the posterior (updated) odds of being a terrorist given the evidence:

Posterior odds of H_t $= \left(Prior\ odds\ of\ H_t \right) \times BF$

Let us now delve deeper into the Bayesian process. First, we must compute the odds of the hypothesis being true rather than the probability of the hypothesis being false. This move has a clear theoretical justification. According to the likelihood approach (Edwards, 1972/1992; Sober, 1990), a hypothesis, *H*, is meaningful *only when compared to an alternative hypothesis, −H*. In general, the law of likelihood suggests that "evidence *E* favors hypothesis *H*1 over hypothesis *H*2 if and only if ($\Longleftarrow\Longrightarrow$) *H*1 confers greater probability on *E* than *H*2 does" (Fitelson, 2007, p. 475). This epistemological stance has important cognitive consequences as it prevents us from computing the probability of a single hypothesis *in vacuo*, meaning decontextualized from other alternatives. In addition, it forces us to reduce the number of competing alternatives (i.e. hypotheses).

Determining the prior of *H* is not trivial, specifically when it concerns the prior that a given object is a needle. Paradoxically, being able to compute the prior for the existence of a needle (e.g. an insider) requires us to first recognize the needle with high precision. However, in order to recognize the needle, it would be preferable to use the prior for the existence of the needle, a requirement that throws us into a vicious circle. Using the odds for the hypothesis does not solve the problem of the prior, but at least we don't have to use a single number but a *relative* magnitude, which at the minimum is 1 divided by the size of the relevant population (*N*). For example, in an organization of 10,000 individuals, the minimal odds for initiating the Bayesian process are:

$$\left(\frac{1}{N} \right) / \left((N-1) \div N \right)$$

Setting such a lower bound for the prior results in the problem previously discussed: the one of the low prior. This problem reminds us of the

TABLE 6.1   Posterior odds as a function of the LR

POSTERIOR ODDS	LIKELIHOOD RATIO (LR)
0.00001	1
0.0001	10
0.001	100
0.01	1,000
0.1	10,000

importance of reducing the size of the haystack. However, this should not be too bothersome when what interests us is the direction in which our belief moves rather than in its absolute magnitude. Let's assume that the LR of a person presenting some kind of suspicious behavior (e.g. visiting a radical Islamic website) given that they are a terrorist may range over the following values: 1, 10, 100, 1,000, and 10,000. As the prior odds for being a terrorist are fixed (e.g. 0.00001), Table 6.1 presents the posterior odds as a function of the LR.

It is rather striking to understand that given the low prevalence of terrorists in the population, even when the LR is 100 – meaning that the odds of observing the behavior are 100 times more likely given that a person is a terrorist – the posterior odds of being a terrorist are still very low (i.e. 0.001). This example illustrates two issues: first, the need to reduce the size of the haystack in order to start with higher priors and, second, the difficulty of recognizing a needle given the low prior. Given the low prevalence of the needle, the prior is so low that even powerful probative evidence cannot significantly change our belief that the object we are observing is a needle. However, and as explained before, the problem is less acute when we think about the process in terms of moving to or from a certain hypothesis.

Let us return to the specific example introduced in Chapter 4. Following the example by Wainer and Savage (2008), the probability of being a terrorist is $p = 0.00001$ and the complementary probability is 0.99999. The prior odds of being a terrorist are therefore:

$$H_t = \frac{P(H)}{P(-H)} = \frac{0.00001}{0.99999} = 0.00001$$

The odds of being a terrorist are therefore extremely low. However, when we get the information that an individual is visiting websites relating to radical Islam, then we can scale our prior beliefs:

Posterior odds $= 0.00001 \times 90 = 0.0009$

The odds in favor of the hypothesis that the individual is a terrorist are still very low. However, notice that they have changed from 0.00001 to 0.0009. This doesn't mean that the individual visiting the sites is a terrorist. He may be a curious teenager, an academic seeking to understand radical Islam, a seeker interested in finding his way, a disgruntled young Algerian from the suburbs of Paris excited by the possibility of redemption, and so on. The only thing that this form of Bayesian inference provides us with is the ability to *rescale our prior beliefs*, given some (hopefully) relevant evidence. Let me further explain and illustrate this idea using the concept of the insider threat.

Candidates seeking to work for the intelligence community are required to undergo a battery of personality tests. Following Snowden's case (see Chapter 1), let's assume that a hiring agency would like to rule out candidates who are morally rigid and have a deep conflict with authority. Snowden was known among his colleagues as "more popish than the Pope." This testimony may be indicative of a highly rigid and non-flexible personality that adheres to strict and uncompromising moral norms. In the area of intelligence, inevitably operating in the gray areas of law and morality, such a personality may not be adequate.

Let's now assume that, having learned a lesson from Snowden's case, the National Security Agency (NSA) designs a short test for screening for the insider threat. The test includes the following three items:

1. Morality should never be compromised.
2. I always behave on a higher moral ground than others.
3. In certain contexts of national security, it is legitimate to be morally flexible.

Subjects are asked to judge on a five-point scale how well each item describes them – or, if we don't trust them to honestly respond to the items (and we should not), then an expert is asked to provide the evaluation. A person who scores above a certain threshold is tagged as a potential insider and others are tagged as non-insiders. For example, disagreeing with the third item and agreeing with the two first items might result in an insider tag. Now, let us further assume that among 1,000 candidates for the agency, only 1% have retrospectively been identified as insiders. The prevalence of insiders in our dataset is low and screening for an insider seems to be a problem akin to finding a needle in a haystack.

When analyzing the diagnostic performance of the test, we may get the results shown in Table 6.2. To measure the accuracy of the test, we may use two measures: sensitivity and specificity (first introduced in Chapter 4). The sensitivity (or the recall) of the test is the number of true positives (TP)

TABLE 6.2   The performance of the insider threat test

	OBSERVATION	
TEST	INSIDER	NON-INSIDER
Positive	9	89
Negative	1	901

divided by the number of TPs and false negatives (FN). In other words, it is the ratio of cases our test has correctly identified as insiders to the total number of insiders. In our case, it is 0.90 (i.e. 9 ÷ 10), which means that our test has 90% sensitivity: it has correctly identified 90% of the insiders as such. Specificity is the ratio of true negatives (TN) – those cases the test has correctly diagnosed as non-insiders – to the total number of non-insiders. In our case, the specificity is 0.91 (i.e. 901 ÷ 990). The accuracy of the test is calculated as follows:

$$Accuracy = \frac{TP + TN}{TP + TN + FP + FN}$$

where *FP* is the number of false positives. In our case, the accuracy is therefore 91%, which is quite impressive.

However, the test also produces a high number of FPs ($N = 89$), a result that has various implications. To explain the implications, we may present an imaginary scenario followed by a question. Let's assume that Snowden's imaginary sister, Linda, is a candidate for the agency and that she has completed the test by answering the three items and scored above the threshold. She is therefore tagged by the test as a potential insider. Given the high accuracy of the test, is it more likely that she is an insider than a non-insider?

To answer this question, we may ask what are the chances that she is *really* an insider? Stated differently, we need to consider the probability that she is an insider *given* the evidence provided by the diagnostic test:

$$P\big(Insider/Test\ result > Threshold\big) = ?$$

The result is 0.09, meaning that the probability that Linda is an insider given her test result is such that it is much more likely that she is *not* an insider. This problem of FPs has been presented before (see Chapter 4), but, thinking about it again here, it may still be experienced as counterintuitive. How is it possible that the test is so accurate and yet that Snowden's sister has such a low probability of being an insider, given her test result?

In explaining what he describes as the "paradox," Sanderson suggests that we should think about a diagnostic test not as a simple and straightforward device for gaining a binary answer but as a process through which *prior odds are updated* (3Blue1Brown, 2020). In contrast with probability, odds concern the *ratio* of positive to negative cases. In the above example, the prior odds of a person being an insider are 10–990 (i.e. 0.01 or 1%). If we have no information about a specific individual's responses to the test items, the odds of their being an insider are 1–99. We may update our prior odds by taking the test result into account. Here, we may use the odds of gaining a test result indicating that the subject is an insider (i.e. the evidence, E) given the hypothesis (i.e. H_I) that the subject is an insider:

$$\frac{P(E/H_I)}{P(E/-H_I)}$$

This LR (i.e. the BF) actually expresses the ratio between the sensitivity of a test and its false-positive rate (FPR):

$$BF = \frac{Sensitivity}{FPR}$$

which in our case is:

$$BF = \frac{P(E/H_I)}{P(E/-H_I)} = \frac{Sensitivity}{FPR} = \frac{0.90}{0.09} = 10$$

It must be noted that the BF can be computed for "negative evidence" as well:

$$BF = \frac{P(-E/H_I)}{P(-E/-H_I)}$$

which in our case provides the odds of observing a non-insider signature (i.e. a negative test result) given that the person is an insider (rather than a non-insider). In this case, the BF is the false-negative rate (FNR) divided by the specificity:

$$BF = \frac{FNR}{Specificity}$$

By multiplying the prior odds that a subject is an insider by the BF, we get the *posterior odds* in favor of the hypothesis that the subject is an insider:

$$\frac{P(H_I/E)}{P(-H_I/E)} = \frac{P(H_I)}{P(-H_I)} * \frac{P(E/H_I)}{P(E/-H_I)} = 0.01 \times 10 = 0.1$$

Given this result, we can update our prior belief that the odds of the diagnosed subject being an insider are 1–100 to the updated belief, which is that the odds are 1–10. The focus here is on the *updating of beliefs* rather than on a simple binary answer. Although the odds in favor of the hypothesis that our subject is an insider are still low, they have been updated in a way that significantly increases our *relative* belief that she is an insider. In this case, we may still hold the belief that the subject is a non-insider. However, positively affirming that she is morally rigid increases our belief in the direction of insider.

At this point, you may be starting to understand one possible way out of the binary trap. Some of our problems result from the physical nature of the world and some from pure chance (bad luck). However, some of our problems and difficulties are caused by the mental traps into which we fall as easy prey. Trying to get a binary and conclusive answer to the question of whether someone is a needle or not is such a trap. In real-world contexts, where we are dealing with risky situations, the "answer" provided by our system is not a one-shot, final, and conclusive verdict with a clear binary outcome. In real-world contexts, the updated belief – that our subject looks much more similar to an insider than we originally believed – invites further steps of inquiry and an incremental process of *prioritization*. In the context of solo perpetrators (see Chapter 1), updating our beliefs in a way that increases our suspicion naturally leads to a stepwise process of in-depth inspection, with heavier resources devoted to more suspicious objects. The energy and resources are allocated in a stepwise and incremental manner in order to confirm or reject the "hypothesis" that someone is an insider or heading toward *being* an insider. While you may think of the binary fallacy as trivial, you may be surprised how non-trivial it is and how difficult it is for some people to think in Bayesian terms.

Under the title "A False Dichotomy," Corner and Gill (2015) checked whether there was a difference in terms of mental illness between matched samples of lone- and group-based terrorists. The motivation for this comparison appears in the first sentence of their paper in a reference to understanding the "motivation and drives" of lone-wolf terrorists. We are led to believe that one relevant "motivation" for being a lone-wolf terrorist is mental illness. The researchers' first hypothesis was that lone-wolf terrorists will present a "higher prevalence of mental illness than group-based terrorist actors."

Indeed, this hypothesis was confirmed, as the authors found that the rate of mental illness was higher among lone-wolf terrorists (32% vs. 3%). So far, there is nothing wrong with this potentially interesting finding. However, it shows a difference and nothing more. The problem is with the conclusion that the researchers derive from this finding and others:

> If mental health professionals were aware of these findings, then screening processes can be carried out by security agencies on patients that present similar antecedents and behaviors in medical evaluations.
>
> *(Corner & Gill, 2015, p. 32)*

Now, what does this actually imply? The reader of the paper might be directed to the conclusion that mental illness is a risk factor for being a lone-wolf terrorist (rather than a group-based terrorist). This conclusion seems to be problematic for three main reasons. First, the first question is how someone becomes a terrorist rather than the secondary question of whether they become a lone-wolf or a group-based terrorist. The research doesn't give us any answer to the question and therefore does not provide any proven way of screening for terrorists or potential terrorists. Second, it is not clear how to move from observed *differences* to underlying *causes* and motivations. Can the difference in the prevalence of mental illness be interpreted as causing some people to become lone-wolf terrorists rather than group-based terrorists? The third difficulty is that what we are interested in is computing the probability of an individual becoming a lone-wolf terrorist *given* the evidence that they suffer from a mental illness. Now, the overwhelming majority of the poor individuals suffering from mental illness do not become terrorists of any kind, and the probability that an individual will become a lone-wolf terrorist given that they have a mental illness is so low that we may wonder what the point of Corner and Gill's finding is, and whether it may have no benefit and indeed may be in danger of stereotyping individuals. These authors could have asked what the probability is of a person becoming a lone-wolf terrorist *given* mental illness among an identified population of potential terrorists. However, the paper does not provide us with the ability to identify this population .... Such disturbing conclusions and proposals as are presented by Corner and Gill seem to result from a lack of Bayesian thinking. As explained before, it is not trivial to think in Bayesian terms and therefore it is not surprising that even qualified academics who are experts in their domain knowledge may be subject to some methodological pitfalls.

In the real world, it is not so easy to reach a clear-cut binary decision. Think about Snowden, for example. He is a tech nerd with clear signs of mental rigidity. However, if you recruit people to work as technologists, then you may want them to be well-organized individuals rather than sloppy workers. As a kind of a package deal, this requirement may be hypothetically accompanied by a relatively high incidence of obsessive–compulsive individuals and computer geeks with an Asperger's-type signature. Thus, you may get individuals who are not only talented but also mentally and morally rigid, like Snowden seems to be. Using "Snowden's signature" for a machine learning (ML) classification algorithm to select employees may therefore backfire.

I became familiar with the idea of the "engineer's silo" when I headed my first big tech project. In my experience, some of the engineers were locked up in their restricted territories and found it very difficult to think beyond the well-defined boundaries of software engineering. In fact, the most talented software engineers on my team were highly organized, mentally rigid, and locked in their territory. I then realized that this is a kind of package deal. If you want serious and well-organized software engineers instead of easy-going individuals whose code looks like spaghetti, then you almost inevitably have to accept that these people will probably be mentally rigid. Snowden-type technologists may have their rigid moral norms but you should not screen them out of your system just because they remind you of Snowden. However, you might track their digital signatures in order to identify whether at some point some of them – probably a negligible minority – are moving in a dangerous direction. Say, for instance, one of your tech geeks is a manga lover. He is excited about *Rave Master* or *One Piece* and eager to share his excitement with other manga lovers on their virtual gathering sites. However, your Manga Geek suddenly starts reading Snowden's *Permanent Record* (2019) and visiting sites describing whistle-blowers and their ways of avoiding identification. Because this person is visiting sites that you have included on some sort of a blacklist, you may increase your suspicion that there is an emerging issue, engage another layer of your cybersecurity system, and launch additional means to improve your "diagnosis" of a potentially emerging threat.

In sum, distinguishing the needle from the rest of the hay is difficult because using a binary system of screening for a rare event is inevitably accompanied by a high rate of FPs, which in most cases is impossible to handle. One possible way out of the trap is to adopt a softer approach according to which we incrementally use evidence to update our prior beliefs. Such an approach invites a multilayered and heterogenous system that collects and integrates various cues in order to recalibrate the priors. Becoming a needle may be a matter of degree until a person reaches a tipping point. The trick is to identify the warning signals in advance and to use them in an operative system that directs you to choose the appropriate actions as your priors change. Rather than finding or not finding the needle in the haystack, we are therefore required to use an incremental process of updating our beliefs and deriving operational steps corresponding with our changing and updated priors. However, the mental trap described above (i.e. thinking in binary terms) is not the only bug we may experience in the needle challenge. Another one is described in the next chapter.

NOTE

1. These terms will be used interchangeably.

REFERENCES

3Blue1Brown. (2020, December 22). The medical test paradox, and redesigning Bayes' rule. YouTube. Retrieved January 19, 2022, from https://www.youtube.com/watch?v=lG4VkPoG3ko&t=968s

Bakan, D. (1966). The test of significance in psychological research. *Psychological Bulletin, 66*(6), 423–437.

Cepelewicz, J. (2019, September 24). To pay attention, the brain uses filters, not a spotlight. *Quanta.* Retrieved January 19, 2022, from https://www.quantamagazine.org/to-pay-attention-the-brain-uses-filters-not-a-spotlight-20190924

Cohen, J. (1994). The earth is round ($p < .05$). *American Psychologist, 49*(12), 997–1003.

Corner, E., & Gill, P. (2015). A false dichotomy? Mental illness and lone-actor terrorism. *Law and Human Behavior, 39*(1), 23–34.

Edwards, A. W. F. (1972/1992). *Likelihood.* Baltimore, MD: Johns Hopkins University Press.

Fenton, N., Lagnado, D., Dahlman, C., & Neil, M. (2019). The opportunity prior: A proof-based prior for criminal cases. *Law, Probability and Risk, 18*(4), 237–253.

Fenton, N., & Neil, M. (2021). Calculating the likelihood ratio for multiple pieces of evidence. ArXiv:2106.05328.

Fitelson, B. (2007). Likelihoodism, Bayesianism, and relational confirmation. *Synthese, 156*(3), 473–489.

Snowden, E. (2019). *Permanent record.* New York, NY: Metropolitan Books.

Sober, E. (1990). Contrastive empiricism. *Minnesota Studies in the Philosophy of Science, 14,* 392–410.

Wainer, H., & Savage, S. (2008). Visual revelations: Until proven guilty – False positives and the war on terror. *Chance, 21*(1), 55–58.

How to Reduce the Size of the Haystack

On Impostors, Cats, and False Positives

7

Why is it so difficult to distinguish between the needle and the haystack? A quite technical paper published years ago – Wilk and Włodarczyk (2008) – sparked my interest in a possible explanation. To explain the main lesson that I learned, I would like to return to Shannon's information entropy (introduced in Chapter 5), but this time starting from the questions that we should ask in order to identify the needle.

Given the uncertainty resulting from the probabilities of the different outcomes, Shannon's measure quantifies the number of questions that we should ask to identify our target. Translated into a protocol, the idea seems to be simple and straightforward. First, identify *warning signals* associated with your target behavior. For instance, the Edy system (described in Chapter 4) uses metadata features such as visiting the websites of radical Islamists. It may be argued that such a behavior is a warning signal associated with a future terror attack. Given a set of warning signals (i.e. features) associated with acts of terror, it seems that it should be easy to identify our terrorists, just as we located our domestic cat (Kitmon) napping in one of eight potential

DOI: 10.1201/9781003289647-7

drawers in Chapter 5. This line of reasoning may remind us of the famous Twenty Questions game, which some of us have played as children. The game is simple. One player, who is known as the "answerer," thinks of an object without sharing it with the rest of the players. For example, they might think about their favorite politician – whom they greatly admire for her struggle to free the "Occupied Territories" (although they strangely fail to question her avoidance of fighting the Chinese occupation of Tibet, for instance). While the answerer thinks about her favorite politician, the other players aim to identify the object by taking turns asking questions that can be answered with a simple binary "yes" or "no." Asking the right questions is the key to winning the game. For example, once we have established that the answerer is thinking about a person, we might ask whether they are thinking about a man or a woman. The answer will be half our solution space, leading us closer to the object. Even if we have approximately 1 million potential objects in our mind, we can reduce this list to the hidden object with only 20 (perfectly chosen) questions.

The same game may be played with our potential needles by carefully choosing the questions or features that may bring us closer and closer to our targets. We may examine, for instance, a set of 1 million names that exist in the Terrorist Screening Database of the Federal Bureau of Investigation (FBI) and start to ask questions, such as did he recently buy a weapon? Has he traveled abroad to a terrorist-supporting country? And so on. In theory, knowing which questions to ask (i.e. identifying the most informative features) will at least halve our search space at each step, providing us with a one bit of information at each crossroad, and finally giving us the ability to identify our single object among a fantastical number of other objects in only 20 steps. This seems like a simple recipe with potentially remarkable results. So why don't we play Twenty Questions with our terrorists? Why don't we use the same game to find the needle in the haystack? Is it merely the shortcoming of not knowing the right questions to ask that is the barrier to success?

According to the lesson that I learned from Wilk and Włodarczyk (2008), one possible source of failure is our inability to differentiate between *localization* and *recognition*. Let me reconstruct their argument. An object is hidden in a system of M cells (i.e. M partitions of the features' space). The cells might be the drawers where the cat is napping or a subset of our features' space where our terrorist is located. Wilk and Włodarczyk (2008) explain that according to the Shannon's information model, locating an object in a simple space is *equivalent to finding the cell containing this object*. Localization is therefore equivalent to recognition. In this context, Shannon's information entropy quantifies the number of yes/no questions required to locate the object in the context of our guessing game. Therefore, if we adopt Shannon's idea of entropy then the most important challenge facing us in identifying or locating an object – whether the favorite politician of our player in the Twenty Questions game, a terrorist in a pile of suspects, or any other needle in a haystack – is the use of the appropriate features (i.e. questions) to split our solution space.

Wilk and Włodarczyk (2008) suggest that there are two alternative forms of search, one of which is clearly relevant to our needle challenge. They suggest that (1) the object we seek may have additional features we should account for and (2) there may be more than one object in a cell, which is a situation in which "one finds the cell with a particle (i.e. object or perpetrator) in it but one is still not sure that this is the right ('true') particle" (Wilk & Włodarczyk, 2008, p. 4810). In the second case, *localization is not equivalent to recognition*. In the best-case scenario, you may locate the right cell where your target resides but may still have difficulties in recognizing it among many other objects. This is precisely the problem we encounter in searching for a needle in a haystack, as, despite its possible localization in a certain cell (i.e. a subspace of the features' space), it is accompanied by too many other objects or people (i.e. false positives, or FPs) occupying the same space. In the example of searching for Kitmon, this means we might find the appropriate drawer but then surprisingly find that the drawer is also populated by numerous other cats, indistinguishable from our Kitmon.

The major insights that I gained from Wilk and Włodarczyk's (2008) paper are, first, that localization is not necessarily identical to recognition; second, that in practice it is *probably not* identical to recognition; and, finally, that to distinguish between the needle and the false objects residing with it in the same cell, we should seek a methodology that can not only differentiate between the needle and the stalks of hay but also between the needle and the false objects ("impostors"). It seems that our main challenge – not an easy one – is to differentiate between the impostors and the real object rather than between the real object and the whole haystack. In other words, our main pragmatic challenge may be in identifying a specific type of cue that can sort the impostors from the true objects. This point is elaborated in the next section, where I elaborate further on an idea introduced in Chapter 6 – the importance of reducing the size of the haystack – and the importance of differentiating between objects residing within the same cell or phase space.

THE JIHADIST AND THE CAT

Chapter 6 presented the Bayesian approach and its relevance to the needle challenge. The physicist Jaynes (2003, p. 91) proposed a nice way of using the strength of evidence to update our prior beliefs. Jaynes (2003) proposed measuring the weight of evidence in favor of a hypothesis (H) by translating

TABLE 7.1 Transformation of the prior odds

PRIOR ODDS	LOG_{10} (PRIOR ODDS)	$10 \times LOG_{10}$ (PRIOR ODDS)
1	0	0
10	1	10
100	2	20
1,000	3	30

the odds-based equation into a *decibel* system, where the prior evidence (i.e. $e(H)$) for hypothesis H (e.g. a needle) is:

$$e(H) = 10\log_{10}\left[\frac{P(H)}{P(-H)}\right]$$

The prior odds are simply transformed through the base-10 log, and this result is multiplied by 10 (see Table 7.1). The logarithmic transformation compresses the large values relative to the small data values, and this form of transformation has a neat cognitive explanation (Varshney & Sun, 2013). The difference between a single tiger chasing you in the jungle and no tiger chasing you is a matter of life or death. However, does it really matter whether 3 tigers are chasing you or 30? The logarithmic transformation is therefore appealing from a human cognitive perspective.

According to Jaynes, the posterior degree of belief in H given the evidence E is:

$$e(H|E) = e(H) + 10 \times \log_{10}\left[\frac{P(E|H)}{P(E|-H)}\right]$$

When the process involves several pieces of evidence, this produces a score that we describe as $Jaynes_H$:

$$Jaynes_H = e(H|E) = e(H) + 10\sum_{i=1}^{N}\log_{10}\left[\frac{P(E_i|H)}{P(E_i|-H)}\right]$$

The use of a decibel system is expressed through the common logarithm with the specific choice of base 10. This means that we convert the odds using a logarithmic transformation of base 10 and multiply the result by 10. Let us assume that $P(E/H) = P(E/-H)$. In this case, the ratio is 1, the base 10 logarithm is 0, and therefore the result is 0; this result means that we should change nothing about our prior belief as the evidence has no relevance. Now let us assume that the ratio $P(E|H)/P(E|-H) = 10$. In this case, increasing the odds by a factor of 10 would result in a base 10 logarithm of 1 and a Jaynes score of 10. Increasing the odds to 100 would make the base 10 logarithm equaling to 2, giving a Jaynes score of 20. Increasing the odds by another factor of 10 would result in a ratio of 1,000, a base 10 logarithm of 3, and a score of 30. Each increase by an order of magnitude results in a linear increase of the base 10 logarithm and differences of 10 points in the Jaynes score. It is important to realize that we can do the same thing without the logarithmic transformation and the use of the decibel scale. These are preferences only, chosen for the abovementioned reasons.

Let's see how this idea can be used in our needle challenge. We first start with the odds in favor of our hypothesis. These odds are simply the ratio of the probability of observing our object (a terrorist) and the complementary hypothesis of a person not being a terrorist. Following Jaynes, who suggested transforming all scores using the 10-base log transformation, we get:

$$10 \times \log_{10} 0.00001 = -5$$

This means that the odds are against the hypothesis that an object randomly picked from the haystack is a terrorist. Updating these prior odds using the evidence that an individual is visiting radical Islamic sites is then formalized as follows:

$$e(H|D) = e(H) + 10\log_{10}\left[\frac{P(D|H)}{P(D|-H)}\right]$$

which in our case is:

$$e(H|D) = -5 + 10\log_{10} 90 = 1.95$$

This means that we have updated our belief from a strong disbelief that a randomly picked individual is a terrorist to the belief that he is a terrorist given the above evidence. What happens if we use more than one piece of evidence? For instance, we may find that posting calls for a jihad on social media is evidence that has a likelihood ratio (or Bayes factor) of 3. When using several pieces of evidence, the general formalism is as follows:

$$e(H|D) = e(H) + 10\sum_{i=1}^{N}\log_{10}\left[\frac{P(D|H)}{P(D|-H)}\right]$$

and in our case:

$$e(H|D) = -5 + 10\left(\log_{10} 90 + \log_{10} 3\right) = 18.77$$

The methodology that I have proposed with my colleagues (Neuman, Cohen, & Neuman, 2019) suggests that we should adopt a negative approach to the needle challenge. Instead of using features that may take us closer and closer to the object in a positive and incremental manner, we should focus on:

1. reducing the size of the haystack and
2. differentiating between the true needles and those that look like them (i.e. distinguishing true positives [TPs] from FPs or impostors).

Let me present and illustrate this idea. ISIS is one of the most notorious terrorist movements in recent history, gaining its reputation through orchestrated and well-documented atrocities such as public beheading. As its publicity increased, it gained more and more popularity and support, mainly from young male Muslims who were recruited through social media and joined the jihad. Now, let's assume that we would like to proactively screen for UK jihadists before they sneak across borders to reach a war zone. According to some sources (e.g. Lister, 2015), the estimated number of UK male citizens who joined the jihad was 700. Given the size of the population of the UK, their prevalence was thus extremely low ($p = 0.00001$). Therefore, the Jaynes score for the a priori belief that a person is a jihadist (i.e. H) in this case is:

$$e(H) = 10\log_{10}\left[\frac{P(H)}{P(-H)}\right] = -50$$

This number represents a strong a priori belief *against* the hypothesis that a person is a jihadist. However, we also know that the jihadists are all Muslims and therefore may seek to ascertain the extent to which the information that a person is a Muslim (D_M) is somehow telling about their likelihood of being a jihadist. Let's answer this question by screening a population of 1 million subjects. Muslims make up approximately 5% of the UK population (Office for National Statistics, 2018) and therefore we should have 50,000 Muslims in our sample. The approximate number of jihadists makes up 0.0002% of the Muslim population of the UK and therefore we should expect to find 10 jihadists and 49,990 non-jihadists among our group of 50,000 Muslims. The posterior belief is therefore calculated as follows:

$$e(H/DM) = e(H) + 10\log_{10}\left[\frac{P(DM|H)}{P(DM|-H)}\right] = -37$$

We can clearly see that, in itself, being a Muslim is *very poor evidence* in support of the hypothesis that a subject is a jihadist. In fact, it is such poor evidence that it emphasizes the fact that the overwhelming majority of Muslims are not terrorists. This is precisely the source of the criticism powerfully raised against ethnic profiling by Wainer and Savage (2008). Chapter 4 discussed this criticism at length in terms of FPs and their accompanying price. However, the question that we are asking here is different. The question is not whether a person is a jihadist given that he is a Muslim but whether being a Muslim should be used as a *preliminary screening cue* to reduce the size of the haystack or rule out non-terrorists. To recall, our task is first to reduce the size of the haystack to help us identify the cell where both jihadists and noisy impostors reside.

Let's say that a hypothetical team of engineers working for the UK security agency MI5 builds an automatic system to screen for potential jihadists through an analysis of Facebook pages. Should they dismiss the evidence that a person is a Muslim when they build the system? Wainer and Savage (2008) are expert statisticians who are highly sensitive to methodological pitfalls. However, the impractically high rate of FPs to which they point in their paper should not be considered an argument against using evidence that is accompanied by a high rate of FPs. The MI5 engineers could treat the information that a person is a Muslim as an isolated piece of evidence and, as a result, totally dismiss the importance of the "Muslim feature," with its extremely low diagnostic value and impractically high rate of false alarms. However, if they were to adopt the softer Bayesian approach that I use in this book, then they would notice that considering the evidence that a person is a Muslim would move their scale of confidence that a person is a jihadist from a Jaynes score of −50 to a Jaynes score of −37. It therefore seems that the MI5 engineers designing this screening procedure should take this piece of evidence into account, regardless of the fact that in itself – and as an isolated piece of evidence – it cannot validly screen for jihadists as the FPs are still such that we are left with a needle in a haystack problem.

When screening for jihadists through a Bayesian hypothesis-testing procedure (with a minor "Jaynesian" twist), given the low prevalence of the target group, *it is almost inevitable that the data we collect will need to work "negatively" from a strong negative score to a less negative score.* As such, this process might be totally dismissed by the argument presented by Wainer and Savage (2008) if considered in positive terms. However, if we consider it in negative terms as a process of reducing the size of the haystack, or the original size of the population, then it may be perfectly legitimate as a phase in the screening process. Ruling out the non-jihadists is no less important than ruling in the jihadists.

While being a Muslim is a significant screening cue that can be used to reduce the size of the haystack in a negative manner, it cannot differentiate between Muslims who are jihadists and Muslims who are not jihadists.

My second proposal is therefore that while the Jaynes hypothesis-testing procedure cannot provide us with the smoking gun that would allow us to identify the perpetrator, it clearly provides us with a way of reducing the size of the haystack in which we are searching. Using a Jaynes-type Bayesian form of hypothesis testing is therefore a kind of reasoning *in a negative manner*. In the above example, it reduces our certainty that an individual is a non-jihadist but it cannot provide us with positive evidence that they are a jihadist. To identify the needle, we must move on to the next step.

IDENTIFYING AND USING IMPOSTORS' CUES

Here is my third proposal, which is that one possible approach to improving the screening process is as follows. First, search for a piece of evidence (D_c) such that:

$$\frac{P(D_c|H_J)}{P(D_c|H_I)} > \tau \text{ and } D_c \neq D$$

where H_J is the hypothesis that a person is a jihadist, H_I is the hypothesis that they are an impostor (i.e. a non-jihadi Muslim mistakenly tagged by our system as a jihadist – an FP), and τ is a given threshold. D is just the evidence differentiating between jihadists and non-jihadists (H_N). D_c, the evidence differentiating between true jihadists and false positively identified jihadists, cannot be the same as the evidence differentiating between jihadists and non-jihadists. Identifying these D_c cues – the "impostors' cues" – is at the heart of the proposed screening procedure.

Let's assume that through the analysis of photos on Facebook taken by jihadists, domain experts have noticed that the jihadists are taking pictures with cats (Mohammad's favorite pet) before traveling to war zones. We may examine this piece of evidence and may find out that among the 10 jihadists in our sample, 6 have taken a picture with a cat. In contrast, among those who are non-jihadist Muslims (49,990 people), 2,500 have taken a picture with a cat. Among the Muslims who haven't taken a picture with a cat, only 4 are jihadists and 47,490 are non-jihadists. Using $\tau = 3$ (Kass & Raftery, 1995), the relevant Bayes factor is:

$$BF_{H_J/H_I} = \frac{P(D_c|H_J)}{P(D_c|H_I)} = \frac{0.6}{0.05} > 3$$

and in contrast:

$$BF_{H_J/H_N} = \frac{P(D_c|H_J)}{P(D_c|H_N)} = \frac{0.6}{0.2375} < 3$$

We can see that the D that a person is a Muslim is telling about whether they are a jihadist in a certain "negative" sense of reducing the size of the haystack by ruling out non-jihadists. However, it is *not* telling about whether the person is a jihadist or an FP (i.e. impostor). In contrast, the D_c that a person has taken a picture with a cat is not telling about whether they are a jihadist or a non-jihadist in general, but it may help to distinguish jihadists from impostors given that we have already reduced the size of the haystack. Now, merging our two different pieces of evidence, we may start screening for jihadists by reducing the size of the haystack. This step is achieved by taking the Muslim cue into account and then by moving from strong evidence against the hypothesis that a person is a jihadist (−50) to a much more skeptical stance (−37). When we examine whether the object has taken a picture with a cat, we may move further to −26. In other words, by combining a piece of evidence supporting H_J over H_N with a piece of evidence supporting H_J over H_I, we have been able to improve our screening procedure by reducing the size of the haystack. We could even extend this procedure by looking for the BF as follows:

$$BF_{H_I/H_J} = \frac{P(D_c|H_I)}{P(D_c|H_J)} > 3$$

In cases where additional supporting evidence exists for this BF, and after screening for jihadists, we can then simply screen out (as impostors) cases where the above BF holds. This is actually the heuristic we, my colleagues and I, applied in our paper (Neuman et al., 2019).

Now let's apply the same procedure to an artificial dataset of psychopaths and the task of identifying a psychopathic needle in a haystack of texts. As texts written by psychopaths are extremely rare, my colleagues and I built an artificial dataset of psychopathic sentences. First, we built a corpus by retrieving 7,000 texts from Reddit (https://www.reddit.com). The average length of each text was 632 words ($Sd = 453$) and they ranged from 173 to 2,685 words. The distribution of the texts by topic is presented in Table 7.2.

Next, and drawing on the meanness dimension of the psychopathic personality, we used a psychopathy questionnaire and other sources to form a set of 100 items expressing meanness. For example:

"I enjoy humiliating others"
"I'm always looking for a good fight"
"Revenge is sweet"

TABLE 7.2   Rounded percentages of the topics' distribution in the corpus

TOPIC	PERCENTAGE
Food	18
Music	20
Politics	22
Sports	17
Travel	24

We randomly sampled 300 texts from our corpus and added to each text six items or sentences from the set of psychopathic items we had created. This procedure generated a subset of texts (N=300) with a clear textual signature of psychopathy/meanness.

Next, we used a content analysis tool, and each text in our dataset produced a vector of 194 features normalized to represent the percentage of each content category in the text (e.g. torment, violence, vacation). In the final pre-processing phase, we randomly split the original 7,000 texts into 3 files, each with the same proportions of texts with psychopathic signatures (N=100) and non-psychopathic signatures (N=2,333). The first file we used was titled L1. Our procedure was built around three phases, as described below.

Learning Phase 1

During learning phase 1, we first measured the median score for each content category of each text in L1 and turned the score into a binary number. If the category scored above the median, then it was tagged 1; otherwise it was tagged 0. We treated each binary score of a content category as D and computed the BF, where H was the hypothesis that the text was one with a psychopathic signature and the alternative hypothesis was that it was a normal text:

$$BF_{H/-H} = \left[\frac{P(D|H)}{P(D|-H)} \right]$$

The first output file was a list of the content categories (i.e. the Ds) and each one's BF score, as computed above. Following some common norms (Kass

& Raftery, 1995), we selected for the next phase of the analysis only content categories that produced a BF greater than 3. In our case, we identified 42 relevant content categories. The seven top-ranked categories were:

1. torment
2. monster
3. ridicule
4. exasperation
5. weakness
6. irritability
7. kill

As can be seen, the existence of these content categories in a text clearly provided evidence for the existence of a psychopathic signature in a text.

Learning Phase 2

In the second learning phase, we used the evidence gathered via L1 and tested it on L2 (the second file of texts). We measured the percentages of each content category in each text and turned the scores into binary values using the procedure described above. We used the BF identified for each content category and applied the following procedure:

For text = 1–2,333
and for D_1 to D_{42}
If $D_i = 1$ THEN compute:

$$JaynesH = e(H) + 10\sum \log_{10}\left[\frac{P(D|H)}{P(D|-H)}\right]$$

where $e(H)$ is defined as:

$$e(H) = 10\log_{10}\left[\frac{P(H)}{P(-H)}\right]$$

which in our case was −13.97.

To test the screening procedure of the above measure, we ranked the texts in descending order and analyzed the top 100 texts. The probability of randomly picking out a psychopathic text out of 100 texts was 0.04

(i.e. 4 texts). In practice, we found 52 texts tagged as psychopaths among the top 100 texts. This was a significant improvement. We selected the top 100 texts for further analysis.

Learning Phase 2a

The aim of this phase was to use the data to build a measure for differentiating between TPs and FPs. Texts that were included among the top 100 cases but were not originally labeled as psychopathic (i.e. FPs) were considered to be impostors (i.e. H_I). All other texts were considered to be TPs (i.e. H_P). We reused all of the content categories, scored the 100 texts, and turned the scores into binary numbers. Next, we measured the BF for H_I over H_P and selected the content categories that (1) scored a BF greater than 3 and (2) were not included in the set of content categories identified previously. We then computed the following:

$$Jaynes_I = e(H_I) + 10 \sum \log_{10} \left[\frac{P(D|H_I)}{P(D|H_P)} \right]$$

For the experiment, we used the third dataset, titled "TEST." For each text in this dataset, we built a vector of content binary values as before. Using the 42 content categories identified during learning phase 1, we computed each text's $Jaynes_H$ score. Using the results of learning phase 2, we computed each text's $Jaynes_I$ score by using the 22 content categories that had been identified in the previous phase as differentiating between TPs and impostors (i.e. FPs). Through the min–max transformation, we standardized our two features (i.e. $Jaynes_H$ and $Jaynes_I$) and scored them on a scale ranging from 0 to 1. We hypothesized that if the impostors' cues identified through $Jaynes_I$ were important for the identification of the psychopathic texts, then we should expect to find that $Jaynes_I$ significantly contributed to the classification of the cases as psychopathic beyond what could be gained through $Jaynes_H$. To test the hypothesis that the impostors' cues were significant, we used a classification and regression decision tree classifier (CRT) with the texts' tag (psychopath vs. non-psychopath) as the dependent variable and with $Jaynes_H$ and $Jaynes_I$ as the only independent features. We applied the CRT using a 10-fold cross-validation. Using $Jaynes_H$ as a single feature in the CRT *didn't identify any psychopaths*. However, including $Jaynes_I$ resulted in 67% precision and 64% recall. Figure 7.1 shows the decision tree produced by the classifier after pruning to avoid overfitting.

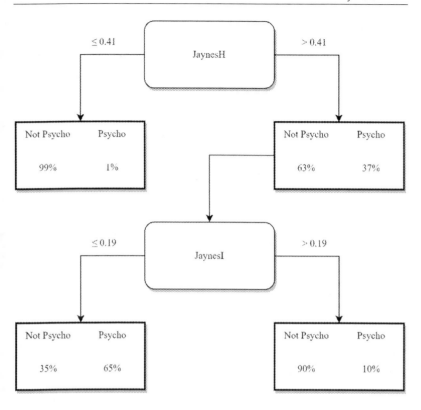

FIGURE 7.1   The decision tree produced by the classifier.

Source: Author.

Let's start interpreting the results by first examining the decision tree. We can see that the decision tree clearly works along the lines provided by our "negative" approach to reducing the size of the haystack. First, it classifies cases as non-psychopathic through the first left branch and correctly classifies 99% of the non-psychopaths, thus ruling them out. If the evidence in support of H_P over H_N is lower than 0.4, the decision is that it is most likely that the text is normal. If the evidence in support of H_P over H_N is higher than a certain value, *then still it is most likely that the text is normal* (i.e. 63%), but here the impostors' cues come into the picture. The classifier takes the impostors' cues into account and suggests that if the evidence in support of the hypothesis that a text belongs to an impostor is higher than a certain value, *then regardless of the first piece of evidence that it is a psychopathic text, 90% of these supposedly psychopathic texts should be dismissed as false alarms.* Thus, it rules them out. However, if the impostors' score is lower than a certain value, then we do not suspect the text to be an FP and we decide that it is a psychopathic text.

This decision tree clearly illustrates the logic presented above, where first the size of the haystack is reduced and then impostors' cues are used to reduce it further. Using impostors' cues significantly reduces the percentage of FPs (by 28%) and significantly increases the precision (by 28%). However, it reduces our recall rate by 10%, which means that we have identified 10% fewer of all of the psychopaths. Here we understand again that we operate in a non-perfect world where a trade-off exists between the prices that we pay (see Chapter 4). However, we have seen some advancement by employing two measures: first, avoiding the simple binary approach in favor of an incremental Bayesian process, and second, understanding that localization is not necessarily identical to recognition and seeking impostors' cues in order to reduce our rate of FPs. Now let's think about the whole process, using an approach that I would like to call *prioritization-based action*.

PRIORITIZATION-BASED ACTION

Let me sum up a few of the main ideas we have discussed so far. We have characterized a needle as:

1. an evolving phenomenon with expected low prevalence,
2. lacking a few simple distinguishable features, and
3. accompanied by the cost of FPs regardless of a test's diagnostic performance.

To address the needle challenge, I have proposed that we should:

1. move from a binary decision to an incremental Bayesian process in which we calibrate our beliefs using informative cues,
2. first reduce the size of the haystack rather than directly seeking the needle, and
3. pay attention to specific cues (i.e. impostors' cues) that may help us to differentiate between the true needles and the FPs (i.e. the impostors).

Up to this point, we have mainly discussed the success of a screening system by using conventional measures such as accuracy. However, let me now locate our analysis in real-world situations, where the success of our systems cannot be measured only through scientific measures gained *in vitro* (i.e. in the lab). In the real world, the success of such a methodology for addressing the needle challenge should be measured *mainly by its practical success in saving the screening efforts of human beings* (Neuman, Assaf, Cohen, & Knoll, 2015) rather than by conventional measures of machine learning performance, such as area under the curve (AUC), precision, or recall. Such a screening procedure may involve:

1. the *ranking* of individuals according to their potential risk, as identified through their signature, and
2. the identification of the top-k subjects and their selection for a secondary, in-depth inspection.

Top-k-ranking methodologies have been intensively studied in information retrieval (e.g. Niu, Guo, Lan, & Cheng, 2012; Zehlike et al., 2017) and appear to be particularly relevant to the needle challenge. A top-k learning-to-rank methodology should be judged on the basis of its ability to identify top-k-ranking potential needles and of the screening efforts saved for the human analyst. Let me illustrate these ideas using the results of a paper that described a way to screen for school shooters (Neuman, Lev-Ran, & Erez, 2020). Together with one of my students and my engineer, I used texts written by school shooters ($N = 18$) and hid them among texts of non-shooters ($N = 5,029$). The prevalence of shooters was very low (i.e. 0.003%) and we tried to see how far we could go in finding the shooters in the forest of normal texts. We used the Bayesian approach detailed in Chapter 6 and ranked the texts/individuals in descending order according to their Jaynes scores. Figure 7.2 presents the percentages of shooters identified within the top-ranked subjects.

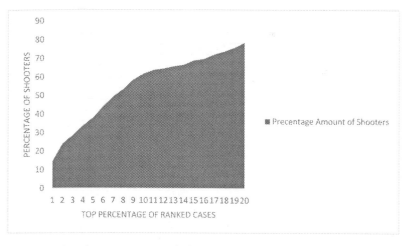

FIGURE 7.2 The percentages of shooters identified within each of the top percentages (1–20) of ranked cases.

Source: Author.

You can see that *the majority of the shooters (i.e. 53.2%) were identified within the top 8% of the highest ranking cases*. Imagine that you are an analyst working for the FBI on an imaginary project called Columbine, named after the Columbine High School massacre. The aim of this project is to screen potential school shooters and to prevent the atrocity of Columbine from being repeated. As part of the project, you have access to the social media of numerous male individuals on some kind of a watch list, and your system rates these individuals based on a diagnostic signature that combines various resources, from criminal records to metadata and Instagram images. If you conduct a top-down screening of the individuals based purely on their ranking, then you will be able to identify the majority of shooters within the top 8% of the dataset – a significant reduction in your workload. Similarly, if you round up the averages, you may be able to identify 60% of the shooters within the top 10% of cases, and you may identify 80% of them within the top 20% of cases. Let's further elaborate on what's happening here. If the screening methodology has a practical benefit, then in each of the $N\%$ of the top-ranked cases, we should expect to find more shooters, on average, than might be found by chance. Figure 7.3 presents the expected numbers of shooters within given percentages of the ranked cases (e.g. the top 1%), and the actual average numbers of shooters identified by our procedure.

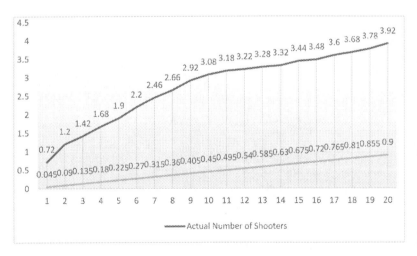

FIGURE 7.3 The expected numbers of shooters within given percentages of the ranked cases.

Source: Author.

Figure 7.4 presents the ratios for the top percentiles.

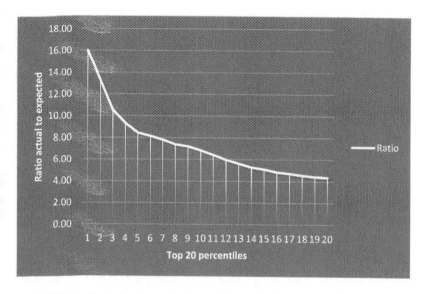

FIGURE 7.4   The ratios between the actual and expected numbers of shooters for the top 20 percentiles of top-ranked cases.

Source: Author.

As can be seen in the figure, the ratio between the expected number of shooters and the actual number of shooters is indicative of the procedure's utility. For example, the ratio between the observed number and the expected number of shooters in the top 1% of ranked cases is 16, which means that by using the proposed methodology for screening the school shooters, the analyst's performance is increased by a factor of 16. This is the major implication of our analysis.

We can see that the ratios range between 16 and 4.36. Therefore, in the worst-case scenario, we can improve our identification of the shooters by a factor of ~4 and in the best-case scenario by a factor of 16, which is quite a lot.

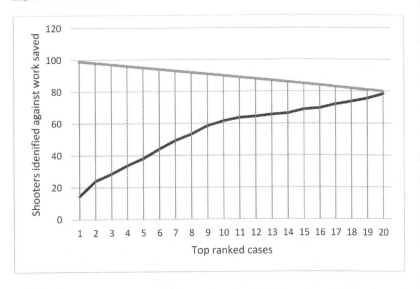

FIGURE 7.5 Percentages of shooters identified (black) against the percentages of work saved (gray) for the top-ranked cases (percentages 1–20) (X-axis).

Source: Author.

We can now return to the results gained through our proposed procedure. A simple illustration of the practical benefits of the methodology can be gained by plotting the percentages of identified shooters against the work saved by the analyst, as presented in Figure 7.5. By adopting the proposed approach, the analyst can avoid engaging in an in-depth examination of 80% of the cases: by focusing on only the top 20% of the rankings, approximately 80% of the shooters can be identified. Similarly, reducing the workload by 90% by focusing on the top 10% of the rankings would lead to the identification of 60% of the shooters. The trade-off is clear – and so, too, are the benefits.

But what does this mean for prioritization-based action? When an analyst is observing a ranked list of suspects, they must allocate resources to the in-depth inspection. Those suspects ranked at the top of the list are approached more quickly than others and with heavier resources. Based on their expert judgment, the analyst then decides whether to move into action. Those prioritized to the top of the list enter an in-depth inspection process where each step, from wiring their phones to arrest and investigation, is performed in a stepwise manner. For example, if an analyst is ranking suspects according to whether they are likely to be insider threats in a technological organization, the analyst may perform a series of in-depth investigations with a team of cyber experts. The team may check whether the top-ranked suspect is doing unauthorized things, such as accessing materials that are not within their scope of responsibility, devoting too much time to reading documents (in a way that indicates suspicious curiosity rather than functional interest), covering their digital footprint, behaving in a way that indicates they are forming an escape plan (e.g. looking for someone who will take care of their pet), or having an anomalous pattern of calls to close individuals (e.g. to say goodbye). In contrast with some paranoid conceptions propagated in the media, people are not equally surveilled. Despite the enormous amount of potential data that can be collected from various digital sources, the bottleneck is such that only an extreme minority of individuals gain such a "special" treatment, and in democracies, such unique attention should be legally approved. A certified herbalist from Boulder, Colorado, who protests against the government's surveillance should be less worried about the government than about the private companies to which he is providing his data for free and with enthusiastic exhibitionism. Some data-based companies seem to profile and track their clients for commercial use much more than the National Security Agency (NSA) tracks innocent American citizens in order to perform a *specific* intervention.

REFERENCES

Jaynes, E. T. (2003). *Probability theory: The logic of science*. Cambridge, UK: Cambridge University Press.

Kass, R. E., & Raftery, A. E. (1995). Bayes factors. *Journal of the American Statistical Association*, 90(430), 773–795. doi: 10.1080/01621459.1995.10476572.

Lister, C. (2015). *Returning foreign fighters: Criminalization or reintegration?* Brookings Doha Center. Retrieved January 19, 2022, from https://www.brookings.edu/wp-content/uploads/2016/06/En-Fighters-Web.pdf

Neuman, Y., Assaf, D., Cohen, Y., & Knoll, J. L. (2015). Profiling school shooters: Automatic text-based analysis. *Frontiers in Psychiatry*, 6, 86.

Neuman, Y., Cohen, Y., & Neuman, Y. (2019). How to (better) find a perpetrator in a haystack. *Journal of Big Data*, 6(1), 1–17.

Neuman, Y., Lev-Ran, Y., & Erez, E. S. (2020). Screening for potential school shooters through the weight of evidence. *Heliyon*, 6(10), e05066.

Niu, S., Guo, J., Lan, Y., & Cheng, X. (2012). Top-k learning to rank: Labeling, ranking and evaluation. In *Proceedings of the 35th international ACM SIGIR conference on research and development in information retrieval* (pp. 751–760). New York, NY: Association for Computing Machinery. doi:10.1145/2348283.2348384

Office for National Statistics. (2018). Muslim population in the UK. Retrieved January 19, 2022, from https://www.ons.gov.uk/aboutus/transparencyandgovernance/freedomofinformationfoi/muslimpopulationintheuk

Varshney, L. R., & Sun, J. Z. (2013). Why do we perceive logarithmically? *Significance, 10*(1), 28–31.

Wainer, H., & Savage, S. (2008). Visual revelations: Until proven guilty – False positives and the war on terror. *Chance, 21*(1), 55–58.

Wilk, G., & Włodarczyk, Z. (2008). Example of a possible interpretation of Tsallis entropy. *Physica A: Statistical Mechanics and Its Applications, 387*(19–20), 4809–4813.

Zehlike, M., Bonchi, F., Castillo, C., Hajian, S., Megahed, M., & Baeza-Yates, R. (2017). FA*IR: A fair top-k ranking algorithm. In *Proceedings of the 26th ACM international conference on information and knowledge management* (pp. 1569–1578). doi:10.1145/3132847.3132938

Needles in the Wild

8

Some Lessons from Nature

I have frequently used the phrase "finding a needle in a haystack" throughout this book, but I have also repeatedly pointed to the shortcomings of the phrase when it concerns human needles. Metaphors may not only be illuminating but they may also restrict our scope and blur substantial differences between the metaphorical domain (i.e. a needle in a haystack) and the codomain that they seek to explain (i.e. an actual search for a "human needle").

One of the main differences between a material object, such as a needle, and a human object, such as a solo perpetrator, is the fact that the human needle is an adaptive system that actively seeks to hide in a haystack. This is a trivial behavior in nature (Stevens, 2016), where cheating and deceiving are common and where objects proactively seek to hide themselves or detect objects hiding from them. In this context, a data scientist seeking to model human behavior for a specific purpose should adopt the guidelines proposed in the seminal work of Luria and Vygotsky (1992), in an essay originally published in the 1930s.

Luria and Vygotsky suggest that there are three intertwined threads that together enable us to understand a human being: the biological evolutionary, which urges us to understand human beings in the context of their wider existence as part of nature; the developmental, which emphasizes the idea that human beings are dynamic systems that change by following ordered developmental trajectories; and the cultural, which points to the fact that human societies have formed complex symbolic systems through which people are guided to behave in a certain manner. According to this perspective, when we truly try to understand the minds of suicide bombers, for instance, we should first try to understand aggression and suicide within the wider context of other mammals. Is suicide observed among animals? If so, in what

DOI: 10.1201/9781003289647-8

contexts? Similarities are important, but so are differences, whether differences of similarities or similarities of differences (Bohm, 1998). Next, we should ask about the developmental trajectory that leads a human being to the decision to die by suicide while also taking the lives of others (i.e. homicide–suicide). Is it possible to identify paths that lead individuals to commit such acts of terror? The cultural thread asks us to identify the cultural schemes through which martyrdom is appreciated and in what contexts, to identify the cultural aspects of homicide–suicide and even to identify those who nurture these cultural schemes. Finding a needle in a haystack is difficult, especially when we are trying to find a suicide bomber. However, if we adopt Luria and Vygotsky's perspective, then a constructive direction may be to target those who propagate the ideal of suicide bombing instead of engaging in the much more difficult task of identifying the needle in the haystack. In metaphorical terms, the idea is to target those who produce the needles rather than to look for the needles themselves. Those who die by suicide may care less about their lives than those who prepare and sending them on their mission, and the "armchair warriors" who preach or financially support the jihad from their convenient seats may care about their lives even more than those who prepare the suicide bombers.

Following Luria and Vygotsky, and starting from the biological evolutionary thread, we may try to better understand camouflage in the natural world. This may give us some insights that can help us to better address the needle challenge and better design screening and diagnostic systems.

In nature, the key to successfully and actively avoiding recognition is *camouflage*, which is grounded in exploiting the observer's psychology (Cuthill, 2019). A psychopath lacking empathy may hide their true nature by pretending to be a benevolent priest. Then, after successfully hiding their true nature, they may exploit the psychology of those that they strive to manipulate. Understanding the mind of the other player in the game is crucial in gaining some kind of advantage, and the first step is to hide your own cards. By understanding people's natural tendency to avoid negative emotions, sophisticated psychopaths may manipulate their victims by evoking strong positive emotions. As a Jewish Moroccan proverb explains, you can drown a person in a bucket of honey, meaning that the end result of a sweet experience might be bitter.

As argued by Cuthill (2019), there are two principles necessary for understanding camouflage: first, the reduction of *signal-to-noise ratio*, and second, that the idea both signal and noise are filtered in *species-specific* ways. These principles have some interesting implications for the needle challenge. We have already seen that a needle is not a simple anomaly. But, in the dynamic and adaptive context of the human needle, we now understand why. The needle actively reduces the signal-to-noise ratio, which means that it attempts to hide its unique signature to avoid recognition. This principle may be applied via "background matching," where the needle pretends to be no different from the background of the hay. The second principle implies that there is no one silver bullet for identifying needles of different sorts. An insider working within a technological organization will probably chose a different form of camouflage from a sexual predator seeking their prey. One of the insights that emerges from these "ecological" principles is that revealing a needle requires a deep understanding of what is being concealed, and sensitivity to what Freud described as "reaction formation" – a form of defense mechanism where unacceptable emotions, thoughts, or behaviors are "mastered by exaggeration of the directly opposing tendency" (Wikipedia, 2022). Once, I watched a documentary film dealing with human trafficking. A first-person testimony by a young girl caught my attention. She told the reporter about the first time she had stepped into the spider's web. She had been sitting in a coffee shop talking to a pimp, and the pimp had just listened to her for three hours. The poor girl confessed that no one had ever listened to her before, and certainly not for three whole hours. Given this situation of apparently full acceptance, empathy, and respect, the girl almost immediately fell in love with her predator.

Now, ask yourself, how many people do you know who would be ready to just listen to you talking for three hours? Some people have the unique talent of temporarily emptying themselves of their ego in order to absorb the concerns of others. If you have ever met such a person, you might like to reflect on your experience of interacting with them. You may have had the relaxed feeling of being absorbed in a sweet cloud. Like the sirens in Greek mythology, they tempt you with their sweet voice, usually in order to gain some benefit. Reflecting on the evidence given by the young girl, I recognized a common denominator between several professions involved in manipulation and the "recruitment" of individuals: pimps hunting young people for sexual trafficking, recruiters for terrorist organizations, and case officers who recruit and operate agents for intelligence agencies. In all of these cases, manipulating others is a tricky issue that must be concealed in some way in order to be fully effective, but the concealment is sometimes evident through the recruiter's exaggeration of the "directly opposing tendency." A stranger who is too empathic, attuned, and generous should immediately raise our suspicion. Similarly, an insider such as Snowden should immediately raise our suspicion given that he was described by his colleagues as "more popish than the Pope" (see Chapter 6). However, this is *exactly* the point where we are misled, because who can doubt the honesty of the teacher's pet? Someone who is more popish than the Pope? Being more popish than the Pope is a masquerading signal and not only a signal that should raise our suspicion.

This logic is deeply related to what I've already explained with regard to the higher variance of a small sample and the way it can be strategically used by the needle (see Chapter 5). By definition, a smaller sample has higher variance (or standard deviation). This means that if we study a very small or even a tiny sample of insiders, then we will probably find that the variance of a measured feature (e.g. conflict with authority) is significantly higher than the corresponding variance of the same feature in the much bigger sample of non-insiders. This higher variance is given but may be strategically used or deliberately formed by a needle. In an insightful paper, Skinner (2011) suggests that in the context of basketball, an underdog team should be willing to take riskier strategies that increase the variance of the final outcome. For example, if an underdog basketball team is competing against a favorite team whose expected score is significantly higher, then, in order to compete with the favorite, the underdog team may pursue risky strategies (such as a three-point shoot from the field). As explained by Skinner, "In quantitative language, the fundamental risk/reward tradeoff for an underdog team is between increasing the mean and increasing the variance of the team's final score" (p. 2). Increasing the variance means that a higher overlap exists between the two distributions – those of the underdog and the favorite.

Similarly, a needle seeking to actively hide itself may benefit from the fact that the variance of its sample is higher than the variance of the haystack. This situation decreases the signal-to-noise ratio. However, by amplifying some of its behaviors – through reaction formation, for instance – the needle may even strategically increase its variance and increase the overlap with the normal group. This is a risky behavior in the sense that the true nature of the needle may be exposed. However, it is a beneficial strategy for reducing the signal-to-noise ratio. There is no need to say that such a strategy may not be conscious or rational/intentional, just like all other evolutionary strategies. If we think about this strategy from a data science perspective, then we may better understand the needle challenge. Let's imagine a scenario where we would like to identify online recruiters to terrorist organizations. These people begin their search for their victims by surfing the net looking for lost souls seeking redemption. Their first encounter with their victim may be characterized by an extremely friendly approach. It is unlikely that they will use words associated with terror, violence, war, or Islam. Understanding this point shows us that we must design a system that looks for other features. The situation is where a lost soul "somehow" encounters someone who is too friendly to be genuine, and our system's features should informatively represent such a situation.

When avoiding a "predator," the needle may use the very same binary fallacy presented in Chapter 6: the predator seeking to recognize the prey can be modeled using signal detection theory. This is a recognition system that must make a decision about whether a signal has reached a threshold indicating the existence of a dangerous object. The counterstrategy that may be used by the needle is to increase the threshold required for identification. The price accompanying suspecting the teacher's pet of being a traitor might be dispro-portionally higher than the one paid for suspecting a less favored worker in the organization. As argued by Scharf, Suarez, Reeve, and Hauber (2020), "The central problem in optimal acceptance threshold theory is to determine what acceptance threshold optimally balances the inversely related probabilities of acceptance errors and rejection errors." Let's assume that suspicion is raised with regard to Snowden. The most rational thing to do is to investigate this sus-picion immediately, as the price of an insider threat is unacceptable. However, organizations and human beings work according to different logics. Suspecting Snowden and inviting him to attend an investigation might lead to him taking offence and quitting his job. A talented systems administrator has been lost, and for what? For a signal just below the threshold? Paradoxically, those we trust the most represent the greatest potential threat to the organization, as a result of their great talent for gaining narcissistic admiration from their super-visors and carefully lowering the threshold for a false alarm.

From the predator's perspective (Galloway, Green, Stevens, & Kelley, 2020), it is important for them to express greater sensitivity to counter the prey's attempt to reduce signal-to-noise ratio. In the context of the solo per-petrator, a higher level of sensitivity means, for instance, that even if a signal has a low level of probative evidence (e.g. being a Muslim), it is nevertheless incorporated into the system for changing our prior beliefs and reducing the size of the haystack. Another strategy used by predators is to use other sen-sory modalities, different from those targeted by the prey. In the context of the insider threat, for instance, the insider may avoid using organizational mail for private correspondence or surfing the net during working hours. In this case, it is clear that other "senses," different from those that are targeted by the insider, must be used to monitor the possibility of a leak. For instance, let's imagine an Islamic terrorist cell operating in the suburbs of Paris. During their training in a foreign country, the members of the cell are cautioned against using their private phones for operative means. Having mapped the cell and the network, we may one day find that the private phones of the three members have stopped working at exactly the same time. Such an anomaly may be explained by a general problem that the local cell phone company is experiencing. However, if this is not the case, we may suspect that the members of the cell are trying to avoid being tracked (i.e. they are targeting our senses) and that they have moved to an alternative platform of communication.

Modeling the needle's mind is therefore a crucial aspect of finding a needle in a haystack. When designing technologies and methodologies for identify-ing needles or emerging needles, designers must be aware of the fact that the needle is an adaptive system that in most cases has no motivation to reveal himself before making its move; that it will actively try to hide itself in a back-ground of "normal" individuals by reducing its signal-to-noise ratio; and that the specificity of its "camouflage" must be taken into account in order to identify the cues relevant to the specific context. The trick is not to be satisfied by simple and trivial evidence. Making an appointment at the Russian embassy in Budapest is clearly not something that an employee of the National Security Agency (NSA) is supposed to do. However, as I have repeatedly emphasized, the competitive edge lies in identifying under-the-radar signals – signals that may be weak and ambiguous but that, when taken together, point to an emerging and disturbing pattern. Reading Snowden's autobiography, we may try to better understand the preeminent signals that may have informative value. His narrative and childhood memoir are clearly indicative of deep conflict with authority figures, as expressed even during his training by the US government. We also learn that his crystallized awareness of the government's "crimes" happened just after he experienced a worsening of his medical condition (Snowden, 2019). Is this a coincidence only? Or is it the case that any form of negatively loaded disruptive change, specifically if it is relational, should increase our concern? To answer these questions, we now move on to the next chapter.

REFERENCES

Bohm, D. (1998). *On creativity* (L. Nichol, Ed.). New York, NY: Routledge.

Cuthill, I. C. (2019). *Camouflage. Journal of Zoology, 308*(2), 75–92.

Galloway, J. A., Green, S. D., Stevens, M., & Kelley, L. A. (2020). Finding a signal hidden among noise: How can predators overcome camouflage strategies? *Philosophical Transactions of the Royal Society B: Biological Sciences, 375*(1802), 20190478.

Luria, A. R., & Vygotsky, L. S. (1992). *Ape, primitive man, and child: Essays in the history of behavior.* New York, NY: Harvester Wheatsheaf.

Scharf, H. M., Suarez, A. V., Reeve, H. K., & Hauber, M. E. (2020). The evolution of conspecific acceptance threshold models. *Philosophical Transactions of the Royal Society B, 375*(1802), 20190475.

Skinner, B. (2011). Scoring strategies for the underdog: A general, quantitative method for determining optimal sports strategies. *Journal of Quantitative Analysis in Sports, 7*(4), 11.

Snowden, E. (2019). *Permanent record.* New York, NY: Metropolitan Books.

Stevens, M. (2016). *Cheats and deceits: How animals and plants exploit and mislead.* Oxford, UK: Oxford University Press.

Wikipedia. (2022). Reaction formation. Retrieved January 19, 2022, from https://en.wikipedia.org/wiki/Reaction_formation.

Lupus and the Needle

9

A Contextual– Dynamic Approach to the Needle Challenge

As if searching for a needle in a haystack isn't difficult enough, imagine that the needle is moving.
(Chiao, 2017)

Given the bounded nature of rationality, our natural tendency for simple heuristics is perfectly clear. Do you remember the story of Little Red Riding Hood? When the little girl faces the bad wolf, who is dressed as her grandmother, she is suspicious and starts asking questions, such as, "Grandmother, why do you have such big teeth?" Her questions are indicative of the features that differentiate between her grandmother and other objects, and more generally between human beings and wolves. Preferring simplicity, we will always look for "the difference that makes a difference" (Bateson, 1972/2000). Having such big teeth is clearly a difference that makes a difference, both for ruling out the possibility that the object dressed in Little Red Riding Hood's clothing is her grandmother and for determining the appropriate action (i.e. run!). However, there are some contexts where identifying a few simple discriminating features is difficult or even impossible. The needle challenge may be one of them, but similar examples exist in other contexts. If we learn about these similar contexts, we may use them as metaphors to enrich our understanding and direct us toward better data science solutions. One of these potentially relevant examples is lupus.

Lupus is an autoimmune disease, which means that our immune system, which is supposed to defend our body from threats, starts to attack the body's own tissues and organs. We can think about autoimmune disease in terms of a deep misunderstanding, where for some reason the immune system fails to differentiate between friend and foe or to recognize real enemies. As a result of this misunderstanding, the immune system starts to attack its own body. Lupus is one such autoimmune disease. It is a vicious condition (mainly affecting women) that attacks the organs and tissues. Despite the visual sign that gave the disease its name – the lupus facial rash – it is difficult to diagnose. In fact, it is so difficult to diagnose that it is difficult to estimate the prevalence of the most common form of this disease, systemic lupus erythematosus (SLE) (Centers for Disease Control and Prevention, n.d.). This is the case because the symptoms significantly vary between individuals, change over time, and overlap with the signs and symptoms of other diseases. As you can see, this is a medical context where the needle challenge seems an apt concept, and we may gain some relevant lessons by delving deeper into the difficulty of diagnosing lupus.

One of the tests used to diagnose lupus is the antinuclear antibody (ANA) test. However, the problem is that while most lupus patients will test positively for ANAs, most people positively tested for ANAs do not suffer from lupus. This is akin to the context of the psychopathy diagnostic test presented before. While most psychopaths lack empathy, most non-empathic individuals are not psychopaths. Lupus is a challenge because there is no *simple and static signature* that would allow us to rule in the lupus cases and to rule out "impostors." In practice, diagnosis is made when at least 4 out of a list of 11 criteria are fulfilled. However, as argued by Cohen (2016, p. 4), "The diagnosis of SLE ultimately rests on expert clinical judgment; but judgment can be less than perfect and even controversial." Given the variability of symptoms among SLE patients, Cohen and colleagues developed a test to rule out SLE. The decision to develop a test to rule out SLE – rather than diagnose it – was based on findings indicating that a patient without an SLE signature "would not be likely to be suffering from SLE," whereas it was not clear whether a patient with an SLE signature would actually be suffering from the disease. This "hard" signature is therefore much more indicative about the *non-existence* of the disease than about the existence of the disease, and these two aspects are *not symmetric*. Ruling out, or reducing the size of the haystack, seems to be an important guideline whether we are searching for a human needle or diagnosing SLE.

Another difficulty is that there is a poor correlation between the signature of SLE and the Systemic Lupus Erythematosus Disease Activity Index (SLEDAI) score, which measures the activity of the disease. This is a surprising finding as, despite the existence of a signature, this signature does not seem to indicate the existence of the disease. Explaining this finding, Putterman et al. (2018, p. 1636) suggest that the six features composing the lupus signature are "not directly involved in the pathogenesis of target tissue inflammation/damage. Rather, the SLE-key test signature is more likely to reflect an underlying autoantibody profile that distinguishes the immune systems of SLE subjects from those of healthy individuals." This interesting interpretation means that the existence of an SLE signature is a distinguishing mark that nevertheless does not entail the existence of the disease. The "hard" signature of SLE may be conceived as a predisposition, like having a predisposition for violent behavior. Such a disposition may have a distinguishing signature, allowing us to rule out non-violent individuals. However, the predisposition does not straightforwardly allow us to predict an outburst of violent behavior or its exact timing. Distinguishing features (i.e. the signature) are not necessarily explanatory (in the causal sense) or predictive. In order to identify when the violent behavior might pop up, it seems that we should identify the relevant context and some contextual triggers. A context may be defined as:

> The relational pattern through which the predisposition is expressed.

We may define contextual triggers as:

> Features that do not differentiate between positive and negative cases but that are associated with the temporal outburst of the behavior

Following this line of reasoning, we can propose a process for identifying the needle, as follows:

1. Ruling-out phase: identify a signature that can rule out true negatives (TNs) and reduce the size of the haystack.
2. Second ruling-out phase: through the use of impostors' cues (see Chapter 7), differentiate between true positives (TPs) and false positives (FPs) in order to rule out the FPs.
3. Identify the context associated with the expression of a predisposition.
4. Identify contextual triggers.
5. Measure the coherence of the relevant evidence.
6. Track the temporal aspect of the indicative features.

Let me explain the above ideas. Imagine a situation where a young man from the suburbs of Paris is imprisoned after being involved in a variety of criminal activities from a very young age. After analyzing his criminal, medical, and family records, we suspect that he is predisposed to violent behavior. In prison, he undergoes a process of Islamization and shortly after being released he starts attending meetings of fundamentalists who call for action against the "enemies" of Islam. A predisposition for violent behavior associated with religious conversion is an emerging pattern that may lead us to prioritize an object (in this case, the young man), and therefore we start tracking his communication network. The object has a signature that differentiates him from TNs, and some behaviors even differentiate him from FPs. At a certain point, we may notice that his relational pattern (i.e. the context) is starting to change and define a new cluster of social interactions. We may represent this relational pattern using a similar approach to the one used in the Groth algorithm, which is used in astronomical observations as well as for the identification of sharks (Groth, 1986; see also Arzoumanian, Holmberg, & Norman, 2005). The object's new cluster of social relations involves convergence toward a very small circle of Islamic brotherhood and divergence from previous social connections with both the criminal world and his close family. When we measure the coherence of features functioning as probative evidence, such as vengeful themes and an apocalyptic sense of urgency on his Facebook page, we may notice an emerging Gestalt (or a picture worth our attention). It must be emphasized, however, that following a Gestalt form of processing is not obligatory. There are some cases where there is no clear Gestalt. Our perception sometimes involves a holistic approach, such as the one used in face recognition. However, in other contexts, we may use an analytical strategy that involves the analysis of isolated informative cues. An increasing rate of change in the needle's sense of urgency may be another important signal that we can track. Given all of this information, a triggering context, such as a personal crisis, may be the spark required to set a fire in this predisposed individual, who is now operating in a flammable context. Notice, though, that a personal crisis is not an informative feature that differentiates between solo perpetrators and non-perpetrators. The overwhelming majority of those who experience a personal crisis, such as separation from a loved one, will not launch a terror attack. However, after ruling out non-perpetrators and separating suspected individuals from impostors, we may find that a personal crisis is associated with an outburst of violence among those we can retrospectively identify as terrorists. However, this contextual trigger appears only when a relevant context is evident.

Through the diagnosis of lupus, we may learn another important lesson. Identifying a needle in a haystack is no less challenging than diagnosing a disease with available tests and reported symptoms in a cooperative patient. The needle challenge does not only involve an adaptive and non-cooperative object, but also a moving target that responds to contextual triggers. I have mentioned the trigger of a personal crisis, but there are other possible triggers as well. For instance, the *copycat* pattern of behavior involves the imitation of criminal activity. A young Muslim may be inspired by the martyrdom of a suicide bomber and follow in his footsteps, just to gain the same perceived glory as his hero. Another trigger for action may be a sense of threat to some kind of an ideological *collective self.* Snowden might have the predisposition to rebel against authority figures, but his reported motivation seems to have resulted from conceiving an urgent threat to the idealized American self, as epitomized by the American Constitution. There seems to be a common denominator to all of these contextual triggers, which is a *threat to the self, whether collective or personal.* A deep personal crisis threatening the self is a warning signal. This common denominator resonates with a simple and integrative theory of personality that I have proposed elsewhere (Neuman, 2014, 2016). An individual predisposed to "needle-like behavior" should therefore be monitored for their perception of threat. A sense of threat – whether, for example, a threat to a person's self-value resulting from divorce or a threat to the collective self as experienced through the perceived violation of religious places – may be an important triggering event for a predisposed individual.

REFERENCES

Arzoumanian, Z., Holmberg, J., & Norman, B. (2005). An astronomical pattern-matching algorithm for computer-aided identification of whale sharks *Rhincodon typus. Journal of Applied Ecology, 42*(6), 999–1011.

Bateson, G. (1972/2000). *Steps to an ecology of mind: Collected essays in anthropology, psychiatry, evolution, and epistemology.* Chicago, IL: University of Chicago Press.

Centers for Disease Control and Prevention. (n.d.). Systemic lupus erythematosus (SLE). Retrieved January 19, 2022, from https://www.cdc.gov/lupus/facts/detailed.html

Chiao, M. (2017). Astrometry: Rise of the machines. *Nature Astronomy, 1*(8), 0191. doi: 10.1038/s41550-017-0191.

Cohen, I. R. (2016). Antigen-microarray profiling of antibodies in SLE: A personal view of translation from basic science to the clinic. *Lupus Open Access, 1*(3), 118.

Groth, E. J. (1986). A pattern-matching algorithm for two-dimensional coordinate lists. *Astronomical Journal, 91,* 1244–1248.

Neuman, Y. (2014). Personality from a cognitive-biological perspective. *Physics of Life Reviews, 11*(4), 650–686.

Neuman, Y. (2016). *Shakespeare for the intelligence agent: Toward understanding real personalities.* Lanham, MA: Rowman & Littlefield.

Putterman, C., Pisetsky, D. S., Petri, M., Caricchio, R., Wu, A. H., Sanz, I., ... & Cohen, I. R. (2018). The SLE-key test serological signature: New insights into the course of lupus. *Rheumatology, 57*(9), 1632–1640.

How to Deal with Tiny Datasets

10

The Power of AI

It's a bird… It's a plane… It's Superman.[1]

A common belief in the scientific literature dealing with machine learning (ML) is that there is an inevitable trade-off between the number of *parameters* used to train a model and *overfitting*. Overfitting is one of the most basic dangers in scientific modeling. Take a look at Figure 10.1, which presents measured level of happiness as a function of time. You may ask yourself whether there is a mathematical function that describes these observations. We can simply connect the dots, as shown in Figure 10.2, and formulate the exact function that describes our data.

DOI: 10.1201/9781003289647-10

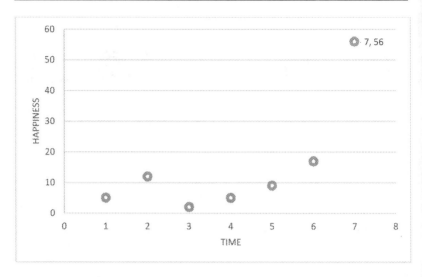

FIGURE 10.1   Happiness as a function of time.

Source: Author.

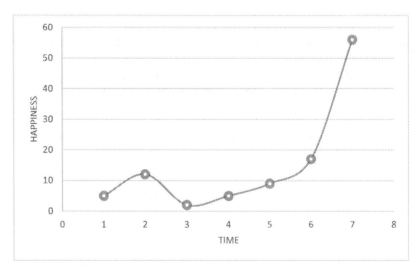

FIGURE 10.2   Connecting the dots of Figure 10.1.

Source: Author.

Connecting the dots using a mathematical function, complex as it may be, is always possible, but at the price of overfitting, meaning that the overfitted function is probably invalid in terms of its ability to describe future observations. Figure 10.2 uses only one independent variable, which is time. However, the more parameters we use, with the accompanying requirement for the corresponding number of observations, the more our model will be prone to overfitting. This is because by using more parameters, we may better describe the behavior by simply using more "coordinates." Surprisingly, this belief, which has its origins in statistics, does not seem to hold for deep neural networks capable of using an enormous number of parameters while at the same time of generalizing beyond the sample on which they have been trained. This achievement of deep neural networks sounds like an incredible breakthrough in modeling and predicting, but some adjustment must be made to use this powerful tool in our context. So far, we've used a Bayesian approach to model the needle challenge (see Chapter 6). The Bayesian approach has an enormous benefit for the *modeler*. Data scientists may use the Bayesian approach not only to model their object's (e.g. an insider) behavior through a well-defined task but also to model their *own* modeling process. In other words, thinking in Bayesian terms has the clear benefit of structuring the way in which we model the behavior of an object using a few features. However, and given the enormous success of deep neural networks, we may ask whether it is possible to use these models for the needle challenge in a way that may somehow complement the Bayesian approach used so far.

Using deep neural networks in relation to the needle challenge is a proposal that may be almost automatically rejected given the small number of observations existing for the needle challenge and the relatively enormous number of observations required to train a neural network. This approach usually requires a large number of labeled cases, which is not always available. To recall, there are several important contexts, such as the needle challenge, in which obtaining a massive amount of labeled data is impossible. In some cases, the small size of the dataset is *inherent* to the context. For example, in trying to build an automatic screening system for the identification of solo perpetrators, such as school shooters or lone-wolf terrorists, the number of cases needed to train a classifier is *inherently* small as these are rare events. In other cases, we may consider extending a small dataset through statistical or human interventions. However, there are some contexts where such extensions cannot be practically performed, such as in cases where the small dataset is highly sensitive (i.e. confidential) and cannot be processed through public outsourcing platforms (such as Amazon Mechanical Turk). Moreover, the deep learning approach is specifically relevant to contexts such as image analysis, where all the information required for an incremental optimization exists in the stimuli. In this context, what you see is what you get, and all that you need for a system to effectively learn a discriminating function is embedded in a reducible stimulus (i.e. one that can be reduced to a large features' space; see Chapter 7) populating a *large* dataset. In contrast, in the context of learning from a small sample, such as screening for solo perpetrators, there is usually much more in the phenomenon that you are analyzing than what you see and get from the data, and inferential processes drawing on external sources of knowledge seem to be a must, in order to test a given hypothesis or reach a decision. For example, while the features extracted from numerous pictures of cats are apparently all you need to build a deep learning classifier for cat images, in the context of solo perpetrators, the available digital signatures are usually not enough to learn the signature of a perpetrator, and you must go *beyond the data* in order to generate hypotheses and make inferences. In sum, some contexts relating to small datasets seem to inherently present different data qualities than those that easily lend themselves to powerful deep learning models. This challenging set of circumstances invites the question of how such processes are performed by natural, rather than artificial, intelligence.

Recent advancements in data augmentation (e.g. Anaby-Tavor et al., 2020) creatively address the difficulty of using a deep neural net for learning from a small dataset, but it is not clear how they can be applied to the needle challenge. While the tiny dataset available to the needle-hunter is definitely a problem, I have developed with my colleagues (Neuman, Vilenchik, & Kozhukhov, 2022) a unique and novel data augmentation approach to model rare human phenomena. To introduce this methodology, I start by explaining the importance of going beyond the data, through the old idea of *abductive inference*. I first introduce and critically analyze the famous *duck test*, which is used to illustrate abductive inference. In doing so, I aim to provide a conceptual analysis of abductive inference. Using this example, we may gain a deeper understanding of abductive inference, understand the importance of going beyond the data, through domain expertise and abductive inference, and see how creative ways of going beyond the data may be combined with current methodologies in the field of deep neural networks to improve our ability to address the needle challenge.

THE DUCK TEST

Abductive inference was defined by Peirce (CP 5.171–172) as a "process of forming an explanatory hypothesis." He explains this process as follows (CP 5.188–189):

The surprising fact, C, is observed;
But if A were true, C would be a matter of course,
Hence, there is reason to suspect that A is true.

This process is far from clear. How do we decide what is a "surprising fact" or surprising evidence? How do we generate hypothesis A? Peirce (W 1:180) also describes the process as follows:

> The inference of a cause from its effect or reasoning to a physical hypothesis. I call this reasoning *à posteriori.*

In Bayesian terms, this process is clear, as it involves the posterior odds in favor of a hypothesis given some evidence. However, the psycho-logic underlying this process is still not clear, specifically if we would like to engineer better AI tools to help us with the needle challenge. Up to now, we have considered a process where the hypothesis is given (H = a terrorist) and evidence is collected to compute the posterior odds in favor of the hypothesis given the evidence. However, the way in which features (i.e. evidence) were identified or hypotheses were generated was not always clear. To gain a deeper understanding of this process of generating hypotheses and identifying features, we will now turn to the duck test, which is sometimes presented as an example of abductive inference. The famous duck test simply states that if something:

1. looks like a duck,
2. swims like a duck, and
3. quacks like a duck,

then the conclusion is that it is probably a duck. In this context, the assumption is that we know what a duck is and that the process of *reasoning from premises to hypotheses* involves some kind of diagnosis that will help us to decide whether something, whose identity is not clear yet, is a duck, as we suspect. This test is like the "What Am I?" guessing game, where a teacher thinks of something and then gives students three clues as to what it is. The duck test is therefore a form of *educated guessing*, which has been described in terms of abductive inference or abductive reasoning (Sebeok & Umiker-Sebeok, 1979). As argued by Bhagavatula et al. (2019), most of the existing work on abductive reasoning has focused on formal logic. Bhagavatula et al. present a deep neural network model for language-based abductive reasoning that relies on massive computational resources. Here, we discuss abductive reasoning from the perspective of cognitive science and by relying on less massive datasets.

The duck test is commonly presented as a form of abductive reasoning and therefore it is important to carefully analyze it in order to clarify the meaning of abductive inference. To understand the process of abductive inference, we may start with the proposition "it looks like a duck." We may then hypothesize that this proposition results from the observation that our object displays a duckwalk – that is, walks in a crouch or full squatting position. The statement "X looks like a duck" is therefore not the first part of our inference process but the result of a *previous* step of observing and conceptualizing a trait or feature (e.g. walking in a full squatting position), relating or patterning it to other observations that exist in our database by asking who or what presents the same trait, and establishing a similarity as expressed by the "like" relation: "X looks *like a* duck". In other words, the first observation (i.e. "X looks like a duck") may be conceived as the outcome of *metric learning* where a distance function has already been learned concerning the objects Duck and X to conclude that "X looks like_a duck." From a more general perspective, we may interpret the process as starting with some measurable features (e.g. a duckwalk) and the identification of objects that are similar to the object in question. However, even this process can take place only after we have identified a relevant feature, which is the duckwalk or the fact that a duck has a beak. This is far from a trivial task even for modern deep neural networks. As explained by Bengio (cited in Heaven, 2019), deep neural networks "don't have a good model of *how to pick out what matters*." Bengio adds that "we know from *prior* experience which features are the salient ones … And that comes from a deep understanding of the *structure* of the world" (p. 165). At this point, we understand that the process of abductive inference, as illustrated through the famous duck test, is much more complicated than its simple presentation might lead us to believe. First, we observe the object and "pick out what matters" (i.e. identify relevant features). Next, we use our knowledge of the world and search our database or memory for objects with the same or a similar property (e.g. beak), and we finally establish a similarity between the observed object (X), whose identity is in question, and one of the objects found through the memory search, an object that is supposed to give us the answer to what X is. This is the perspective of high-level cognition that I adopt for the current discussion. It doesn't contradict models of deep learning but invites us to approach the problem of small datasets from a specific theoretical approach. The lesson we may learn so far is that we must (1) identify relevant features of the object and (2) somehow use them to extend our knowledge of its features and those objects that are characterized by them. These two points will be elaborated in the next section in an analysis of the case study of a solo perpetrator.

It must be noted that the proposition "X looks like a duck" cannot be used as conclusive evidence that X *is a* duck, as moving from *similarity* (i.e. X is like Y) to *identity* (i.e. X is Y), or even to the hypothesis (*H*): X is Y, is not trivial. The fact that something looks like a duck doesn't mean it is a duck. Rather than a duck, it may be Groucho Marx, whose signature walk was the duckwalk. The example of Groucho Marx is important as it explains that the amusement we may experience while watching Groucho Marx in movies such as *Duck Soup* (1933) doesn't result from the uncertainty as to whether Groucho Marx is a human being or a duck, but from the fact that despite the certainty that Groucho Marx is a human being, he *looks like* (i.e. similar to) a duck, and this similarity is amusing.

To explain how the first proposition (i.e. "X looks like a duck") is produced, we may use a simpler example and interpret it as resulting from the observation that our object has a beak. Given this piece of data or evidence (i.e. E), we may search a given dataset (e.g. ConceptNet) to identify the set of objects (i.e. Hypotheses) possessing this property and by including by default a new object (H^*) that doesn't exist in our database but that may be used as a default hypothesis when other hypotheses are either missing or cannot be selected through evidential support. Using this procedure, we may find that a beak is a property of ducks, falcons, eagles, and many other objects semantically mostly grouped under the category of bird. Identifying similar objects and their semantic categories involves basic cognitive processes of comparison and abstraction. Using this procedure, we can assign each identified feature of the observed object to a set of objects that all have the same feature and that may serve as potential hypotheses to be tested.

Moving to the next proposition, "it swims like a duck," we may interpret it as resulting from the observation that our object (1) swims and (2) swims *effortlessly*. Searching Google for objects associated with "swimming effortlessly," we identify as our first objects whales, seals, ducks, and swimmers involved in the total immersion swimming method. All of these objects and their categories (e.g. bird) are marked as hypothetical candidates for the identity of the observed (or concealed!) object.

A last proposition involves the verb "quack," which can be interpreted as the act of making a harsh sound unique to a duck. This is the most important feature, as only a duck quacks. In fact, we could have used this cue alone. Given the above pieces of data and the objects hypothesized through our search process to have these traits, we may collapse the objects into several top-level semantic categories (e.g. a person). In this way, we will see that the number of potential hypotheses generated by the search process and supported by the evidence is basically *limited*. In sum, first, we identify the features characterizing our object (e.g. quacks or swims effortlessly); next, we search for objects characterized by these features and identify the categories to which these objects belong; and finally, we compute the likelihood of one hypothesis over the other (e.g. duck over swimmer) to select the leading hypotheses or to sort out the hypotheses (rankings) and reach a conclusion.

As the likelihood approach to statistical inference (Edwards, 1972/1992, p. 1) involves the assessment of "the relative merits of rival hypotheses in the light of observational or experimental data," we may reconstruct the abovementioned inferential process through which the hypotheses (that our observed object looks, swims, and quacks like a duck) are generated and integrated into the final hypothesis that our object is a duck. However, it must be noted that the duck test doesn't easily lend itself to a Bayesian form of analysis as we have no way of determining the a priori strength of our belief that the observed object is a duck (i.e. $P(Duck)$) even at the stage of drawing the similarity relation "X looks like a duck." In fact, the Groucho Marx example illustrates the irrelevance of such a move both theoretically and practically, as the hypothesis that X is a duck is not a priori given but generated through the similarity, which doesn't lead in any trivial way to assigning the hypothesis a number expressing our degree of belief.

An important aspect of this measure of evidential support is that it is *indifferent to the prior belief for H* and the appropriate way to compute it, which is one of the headaches facing Bayesian inference. In the case of the duck test, given that it is an abductive form of inference, we should not be bothered by determining the a priori degree of belief that our object is a duck. The only important point is the Bayes factor (BF), or likelihood ratio, through which we can agree on how much of a "difference" E makes for H. As our mind is basically relational (Neuman, 2017), computing the "difference that makes a difference" (Bateson, 1972/2000), through the BF, can be done heuristically. For instance, it is quite difficult to imagine that, given their limited cognitive resources and bounded rationality, human beings will be able to easily and validly compute:

$$K = \frac{P(\text{Beak/Bird})}{P(\text{Beak/Not } Bird)}$$

In addition, it is not clear how to identify the complementary hypothesis, $-H$. How do we decide what is $-H$? This is a crucial issue. If E = Beak then H = Duck, but what is the complementary hypothesis, $-H$? What is this non-bird? A mammal? The solution space to $-H$ is potentially infinite. Luckily, the constraints operated by real-world constraints significantly reduce the space of the potential hypotheses. Here this problem is solved by identifying the objects that share features with our object, and their categories. Given the few high-level categories that we've identified, the problem of identifying $-H$ can be heuristically addressed. Moreover, the ratio between these two quantities can be heuristically estimated so as to exclude rare cases (e.g. the platypus) or metaphorical usages of language. Following the idea that small samples may have a cognitive benefit (Kareev, 1995), we may use Google Search to retrieve the first seven images using the keyword "beak." The images I've identified were bird, toucan, squid, eagle, parrot, duck, and chicken. The ratio between bird images and non-bird images is such that the BF of:

$$BF = \frac{P(E = \text{Beak}/H = \text{Bird})}{P(E = \text{Beak}/-H)}$$

can be approximated according to the ratio of duck to non-duck objects.

Up to now, I've explained the abductive inference approach at a very general and high level, but what has it to do with the needle challenge? My use of an abductive inference approach is illustrated and further explained in the next section.

LEARNING FROM A SINGLE CASE OF A SOLO PERPETRATOR

Seung-Hui Cho was the perpetrator responsible for the Virginia Tech Shooting, where 32 innocent individuals lost their lives and 23 were injured. Cho sent his "manifesto" to the media to explain the reasons for his behavior, and this document provides us with a window into the mind of a disturbed and dangerous individual. Although it is a single case, we may use it, as I have repeatedly done in various papers (e.g. Neuman, 2019), to show how a general lesson may be learned from a single case. Let me illustrate how, through the lessons we have learned about abductive inference, we may be able to perform a process of general abstraction through the analysis of a case study.

The manifesto opens with the following lines:

> Oh the happiness I could have had mingling among you hedonists, being counted as one of you, only if you didn't fuck the living shit out of me.

In response to the question of how to pick out what matters (see Bengio's criticism as presented earlier in this chapter), we can propose the following guidelines. As the manifesto concerns human beings, it is important to examine their beliefs about themselves (e.g. "I feel lonely and depressed") and their beliefs about others (e.g. "Your friends can never be trusted"). Therefore, our attention should be directed to "what matters" (i.e. relations between self and others) in order to "pick out" the relevant features associated with beliefs about self and others. With this theoretical guideline, we notice that in his opening paragraph, Cho describes his victims using the noun "hedonists" and describes the basic relation between himself and others in terms of blame; those he addresses are accused of (or blamed for) "fuck[ing] the living shit out of [him]." In this context, we may ask the following questions:

1. If someone is a hedonist, what else can be said about them?
2. Who are the objects described as "hedonists"?
3. Which objects might "fuck the living shit" out of someone?
4. What kind of object is being fucked?
5. If someone "fucks the living shit" out of someone, what else can they do to that person?

More generally, we are seeking:

- to "embed" the attributes of self and others,
- to identify the objects associated with these attributes, and
- to understand the relations associated with these objects.

In other words, in this single case study, we are seeking to *guess* more about the objects and relations that appear in the text. Using iWeb,[2] a 14-billion-word corpus, we can input the word "hedonist" and identify the *negatively* loaded adjectives co-located with our word. This means that in order to better understand the meaning of the attribute used by Cho to describe others, we can simply use a very large corpus to identify the negatively loaded adjectives associated with the attribute. The top three words associated with "hedonist" on iWeb are "selfish," "egoistical," and "amoral." We may hypothesize that our perpetrator conceived his victims not only as "hedonists" but also as selfish, egoistical, and amoral. This is a guess or hypothesis we have formed through the text and the use of external resources. Even this preliminary hypothesis may be used to build a hypothetical signature of the needle (i.e. in this case, a solo perpetrator). What can we say about a person who conceives others as hedonistic, selfish, egoistical, and amoral? Who are these people? To whom are they similar? What can we expect them to do?

Later Cho describes his victims as "sadistic." Using the same procedure, the top three negatively loaded adjectives collocated with this word are: "cruel," "brutal," and "violent." Using simple technologies to measure the semantic similarity between vectors (or arrays) of words, we may discover that [selfish, egoistical, amoral] is associated with [cruel, brutal, violent]. Now, through this updated hypotheses that those Cho describes as sadistic are also cruel, brutal, and violent, we may ask the same question as before. Who are these people and what can we expect of them? If we check iWeb for objects described as sadistic, we may identify human objects such as killers, psychopaths, and... dentists. You may be surprised that dentists are described as sadists, but recall the 2005 film version of *Charlie and the Chocolate Factory*, where the hero's father is a quite vicious dentist who treats his son in a painful way. Killers, psychopaths, and dentists have a common denominator, which is inflicting pain. Cho, the perpetrator, conceived his victims in an overgeneralized way as those who had inflicted pain on him, and his violent aggressive act may paradoxically be understood as an act of defense against aggressors.

Using this simple process of abductive inference, we may start to generate hypotheses about the mind of the perpetrator and the way he conceives himself and others. We may try to reconstruct his worldview and the ways in which he conceives himself (e.g. a victim) and others (e.g. offenders). For example, we may guess that Cho conceives his victims as aggressors, who are similar to killers and psychopaths, or to people who inflict pain on others (e.g. dentists). Moreover, the hypotheses may be tested for coherence within the same text. One of the objects associated with hedonists in iWeb is "French." However, this object (i.e. French people) is not coherent (i.e. associated) with the other objects obtained through the analysis of Cho's manifesto, as attributes such as "sadistic" and "brutal" are not informatively associated with "French." Therefore, the hypothesis that the objects (i.e. others) similar to Cho's victims include the French people should be eliminated in favor of a much more likely hypothesis: that he conceived those he harmed not as innocent victims but as aggressors who inflicted pain on others, including Cho himself.

Using this simple proposed strategy of abductive inference, we may generate and test hypotheses even with regard to a single case study. For example, we may hypothesize that deep psychological pain, a sense of victimhood, and overgeneralization of others as aggressors may be warning signs of a school shooter. Here, I would like to emphasize the important point that the whole process of abductive inference described so far aims to serve the domain expertise of the researcher seeking to "augment" his small sample in order to build a screening system. Whether the disturbed mind of Cho is representative of all, or most, solo perpetrators is an open question, but at least we have a starting point for creating a "warning profile" of a disturbed and dangerous individual with no theoretical predispositions forced top-down on the needle. The same procedure may be applied to a small sample of individuals, and through comparing and contrasting, we may better understand the character of the needle and produce much more efficient tools for identifying it in the haystack. However, this is only a preliminary stage for the data analyst as the ability to "guess" has recently been significantly improved through the introduction of transformers. Transformers may be a turning point in our ability to use tiny datasets in the context of the needle challenge. They do not undermine the process described so far. On the contrary, they may powerfully complement that process by allowing us to generate synthetic data out of tiny datasets. This synthetic data may be used by powerful deep neural networks to help us to address the needle challenge. The next section introduces this novel idea.

ABDUCTIVE INFERENCE THROUGH TRANSFORMERS

Transformers are deep neural networks that automatically produce a state-of-the-art representation of a sequence of data through a mechanism known as "attention." These models – epitomized by GPT-3 (Brown et al., 2020) – are sometimes presented as a new form of AI, but we have to understand that they are excellent at performing at a very specific task, which is the completion of a masked token (or series of tokens) in a sequence. For example, I can present to a model the following question, which it has never been exposed to before or learned how to answer: "I like to eat fish and ___?" Guessing the missing token is the model's *raison d'être*, or its basic justification. In its attempt to guess the missing token, the model may propose several reasonable suggestions, such as "chips." Although a specific individual may like to eat fish and ice cream, this is a less probable choice. Through being trained on a huge dataset of texts, the model learns the deep and contextual connections between the meanings of words, in a way that may be used to guess a masked (i.e. hidden) token or a sequence of tokens. Despite the hype surrounding GPT-3, it is clearly accompanied by difficulties (e.g. Marcus & Davis, 2020) that set clear boundaries around the technology and some of its pretensions. On the other hand, it is an extremely powerful tool for those who know how to converse with the machine through the appropriate prompting of data and fine-tuning the model through the learning phase.

As the transformer is a promising tool for those who are struggling with a lack of data when trying to address the needle challenge. The next section presents the way in which, together with my colleague Dan Vilenchik and our student Vladislav Kozhukhov, I have used the GPT-2 model to produce high-quality synthetic data for modeling a rare personality disorder. It must be noted that this is a promising technology because it allows us to model the mind of another human being even if we lack sufficient data for the personality type that we seek to model. Moreover, we can use the model to indirectly question an individual about specific things that we find interesting. Think, for example, about the insider threat, and imagine that we are interviewing a candidate for a sensitive position. If the candidate is asked a question whose answer may have negative consequences, then most likely they will not answer it truthfully. When people are interviewed or asked to fill in a questionnaire, we assume that they are *reflective* and *honest*. They should be reflective enough to know themselves and accurately report their mental state, and honest enough to share this information with others. However, these assumptions are not realistic. Most people that we meet are not reflective, and their willingness to honestly report their thoughts, emotions, and behaviors is context dependent, meaning that in some contexts people will avoid honestly sharing their emotions, thoughts, and behaviors. This tendency is usually trivial, resulting from people's desire to gain some benefit or to protect their "face" (i.e. their positively presented self). The problem is more acutely expressed in the case of the insider threat. After all, which insider would like to reveal themselves as such? However, imagine a situation where, given enough data, we may build a model of the specific individual – Snowden, for instance. Then, instead of asking the real Snowden direct questions that might incriminate him, we could address the same questions to Snowden's artificial twin, which would lack the ability to lie but would still honestly answer the questions. In this case, I hypothesize that the answers we would get from the twin would be much more honest than those we could get from the original. The general methodology for modeling a given personality, even if we lack substantial data, is presented in the next section.

THE DEXTER MACHINE

Let's say that you are interested in developing a technology for screening psychopaths. If you sought the advice of ML and natural language processing experts, their advice would probably be simple. First, collect the data of confirmed psychopaths; second, train a classifier on the labeled data; and, finally, test the performance of your model. As such, your first challenge is to put your hand on high-quality data. This is far from trivial. First, and as explained below, the prevalence of psychopaths is low. Second, given the bad reputation of psychopaths, a person has to be totally unreflective to expose their dark side. Good luck with finding high-quality data. Third, the "ecological validity" of your dataset may be low, meaning that your ability to use the model beyond the specific context on which it has been trained will probably be low. For instance, it is not clear how data collected on computer trolls may be used to measure the antisocial psychopathic trait among potential cases officers of the Central Intelligence Agency (CIA). Even more basic attempts to measure the correlation between cybercrime and psychopathy may be a challenge, as such studies may mostly be based on non-representative samples that involve self-selection and other sources of bias. After all, no one really checks the personalities of those working for cybercrime organizations from Iran to North Korea.

The lack of high-quality data is not the only challenge. A deeper challenge is to move from *classification* to the *modeling* of human personality. Classification involves the use of certain features in the most optimal way to sort out the labeled cases. However, classification is limited as it relies too deeply on the features and the classificatory function. For example, let's assume that we are interested in automatically sorting men from women based on their purchasing patterns. A single feature, such as buying tampons, may be all we need (some men buy tampons for their wives or daughters, but still this single feature may be enough). Buying tampons may be a discriminatory feature, but it doesn't explain to us what it means to be a man or a woman. Indeed, using tampons may be a part of being a woman, in specific cultures of course, but it is *a discriminatory and not an explanatory feature*. Similarly, we may notice that listening to rap music is a discriminatory feature between extraverts and introverts (Neuman, Perlovsky, Cohen, & Livshits, 2016), and for a good reason, as discussed in the cited paper. However, being able to sort extraverts from introverts, based on informative features, is not the same as modeling their personalities. Modeling is a top-down process where we try to represent something using a few dimensions representing the core or the essence of what we seek to model. A top-down modeling process combined with the technological promise of the transformer may be the right direction to take. Let me try to illustrate this point.

To model the psychopathic mind, my colleagues and I (Neuman et al., 2022) first adopted a modeling approach relying on the current psychodynamic approach (Lingiardi & McWilliams, 2017), where two main dimensions of personality are (1) beliefs a person holds about themselves and (2) beliefs about others. We then moved on to a data collection phase. As naturally occurring psychopathic texts are extremely rare (as already explored in Chapter 7), we first used Reddit discussion groups dealing with psychopathy (r/psychopath, r/sociopath, and r/antisocial). Although these were not necessarily texts from authenticated psychopaths, they at least dealt with the theme of psychopathy, and we were able to use them as a starting point. After downloading the texts, we cleaned them of spam, hyperlinks, and emojis and removed duplicates. This was our basic corpus. However, to fine-tuning our system, we used texts produced by three fictional psychopathic characters: the Joker (from the 2019 film), Patrick Bateman from *American Psycho* (2000), and Dexter Morgan from the TV series *Dexter* (2006–2013). As the psychopathic mind (Lingiardi & McWilliams, 2017) can be represented through the psychopath's beliefs about themselves (i.e. beliefs about self) and their beliefs about others (i.e. beliefs about others), we used my domain expertise and abductive inference and prepared a list of 20 items representing beliefs about self and 20 items representing beliefs about others. Here are three examples of items concerning beliefs about self:

1. I take advantage of others whenever I can.
2. I experience no remorse for harm or injury I have caused to others.
3. I enjoy manipulating others' emotions to get what I want.

And here are items illustrating beliefs about others:

1. People are selfish.
2. Human beings are greedy.
3. The majority of people are cruel.

We first fine-tuned the GPT-2 transformer to the Reddit data and then to the data of the fictional characters. Next, we used the 40 seed items. For each sentence, we asked the transformer to do what it is good at and to produce for each sentence 200 sentences succeeding it in a semantically meaningful manner. The problem, as expected, was that the transformer generated too much garbage. Therefore, we cleaned the data and used a methodology to rank the sentences according to their similarity to a psychopathic vector (i.e. an array of words representing psychopathy). Selecting the top-ranked sentences led to a list of around 1,700 sentences supposedly representing the psychopathic mind. These were sentences that did not exist *in vivo*; they were not taken from any real psychopaths. They were sentences produced by the computer that modeled the psychopathic mind with our assistance. These synthetic sentences included the following examples for beliefs about self:

- I kill animals, I rape women, I rob people, I hurt my family.
- I've been arrested, and I've been in trouble with the law for my stupidity.
- I have no remorse for hurting my dog or my cat.

And they included the following examples beliefs about others:

- The majority of people are assholes and not worth the trouble.
- I don't really trust anyone.
- I have been through things that would make a normal person cry.

Not all of the sentences expressed a clear or characteristically psycho-pathic dimension. Some of them touched on aspects of the psychopathic personality and some of them were just noise produced by the transformer, which is just a general and probabilistic model of language. We called our model Dexter.

As the proof is in the pudding, we checked the quality of our synthetic data using cross-domain validation. We first tested our synthetic data by using a dataset of sexual predators (Inches & Crestani, 2012). We chose this dataset because being a sexual predator is correlated with psychopathy. Our first hypothesis was that if the synthetic data generated by Dexter validly represented the psychopathic mind, then they could be used to differentiate between sexual predators and non-predators. Using a BERT (Bidirectional Encoder Representations from Transformers) classifier trained on our artificial data, we scored each individual in the dataset according to what we called their *Psycho*Score. The average scores of predators and non-predators are presented in Figure 10.3.

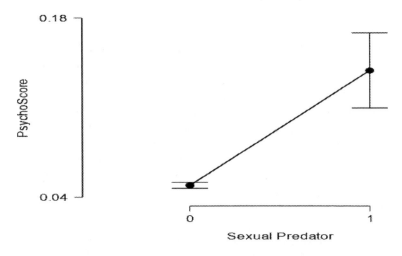

FIGURE 10.3 The *Psycho*Scores of sexual predators versus non-predators.
Source: Author.

As you can see, sexual predators scored significantly higher than non-predators. Moreover, when testing the classification performance of the model and comparing it to other models, we found that our model performed the best, with 84% precision and 75% recall, and our improved models even performed better. This means that although our basic model was *not* trained on the corpus of sexual predators, and although it was not directly related to sexual predators, it was able to identify 75% of the predators in the test set and, when it tagged a subject as a predator, was correct in 85% of the cases. This result and others that we present in our paper (Neuman et al., 2022) show that even when a large dataset is unavailable, we can still use creative ways to model the needle, generate synthetic data, and use the power of advanced technologies to address the needle challenge. By acting as an automated "guesser," the transformer can be used for abductive inference and to generate synthetic data for training a neural network. However, the idea of abductive inference and the way in which it can be used with advances in AI is richer than is described in this chapter, which is only an appetizer.

NOTES

1. From the 1966 musical of that name.
2. See https://www.english-corpora.org/iweb.

REFERENCES

Anaby-Tavor, A., Carmeli, B., Goldbraich, E., Kantor, A., Kour, G., Shlomov, S., ... & Zwerdling, N. (2020). Do not have enough data? Deep learning to the rescue! *Proceedings of the AAAI Conference on Artificial Intelligence, 34*(5), 7383–7390.

Bateson, G. (1972/2000). *Steps to an ecology of mind: Collected essays in anthropology, psychiatry, evolution, and epistemology.* Chicago, IL: University of Chicago Press.

Bhagavatula, C., Bras, R. L., Malaviya, C., Sakaguchi, K., Holtzman, A., Rashkin, H., ... & Choi, Y. (2019). Abductive commonsense reasoning. ArXiv:1908.05739.

Brown, T. B., Mann, B., Ryder, N., Subbiah, M., Kaplan, J., Dhariwal, P., ... & Amodei, D. (2020). Language models are few-shot learners. ArXiv:2005.14165.

Edwards, A. W. F. (1972/1992). *Likelihood.* Baltimore, MD: Johns Hopkins University Press.

Heaven, D. (2019). Why deep-learning AIs are so easy to fool. *Nature, 574*(7777), 163–166. doi: 10.1038/d41586-019-03013-5.

Inches, G., & Crestani, F. (2012). Overview of the international sexual predator identification competition at PAN-2012. In *CLEF (Online Working notes/labs/workshop),* vol. 30. Retrieved January 19, 2022, from https://pan.webis.de/downloads/publications/papers/inches_2012.pdf

Kareev, Y. (1995). Through a narrow window: Working memory capacity and the detection of covariation. *Cognition, 56*(3), 263–269. doi: 10.1016/0010-0277(95)92814-G.

Lingiardi, V., & McWilliams, N. (Eds.). (2017). *Psychodynamic diagnostic manual: PDM-2.* New York, NY: Guilford Press.

Marcus, G., & Davis, E. (2020). GPT-3, Bloviator: OpenAI's language generator has no idea what it's talking about. *Technology Review*. Retrieved January 19, 2022, from https://www.technologyreview.com/2020/08/22/1007539/gpt3-openai-language-generator-artificial-intelligence-ai-opinion

Neuman, Y. (2017). *Mathematical structures of natural intelligence*. New York, NY: Springer.

Neuman, Y. (2019). Language mediated mentalization: A proposed model. *Semiotica*, *2019*(227), 261–272.

Neuman, Y., Perlovsky, L., Cohen, Y., & Livshits, D. (2016). The personality of music genres. *Psychology of Music*, *44*(5), 1044–1057.

Neuman, Y., Vilenchik, D., & Kozhukhov, V. (2022). Data augmentation for modeling human personality: The Dexter machine. Manuscript under review.

Sebeok, T., & Umiker-Sebeok, J. (1979). "You know my method": A juxtaposition of Charles S. Peirce and Sherlock Holmes. *Semiotica*, *26*(3–4), 203–250. doi: 10.1515/semi.1979.26.3-4.203.

Concluding Discussion

11

Isolated Lights in the Abyss of Ignorance

> *What we perceive are no more than isolated lights in the abyss of ignorance.*
> *(Sebald, 1998, p. 19)*

There are some contexts where we encounter phenomena with low prevalence and with only a few simple distinguishable features. When we try to produce a binary diagnosis of a human object and to decide whether it belongs to the minority class in which we are interested, this process is usually accompanied by an impossible price of false alarms, regardless of our test's diagnostic performance (i.e. accuracy). This is the needle challenge, which is the focus of the current book, and the challenge in accompanied by ethical issues as well. For example, the needle may be a whistleblower or a rebel against a tyrannical regime. Seeking a needle in a haystack therefore presents the same challenge to those who are seeking good as it does to those working on behalf of evil regimes, from North Korea to Iran. However, the challenge is substantially more difficult in open societies, where there is sometimes confusion over whether there is a line separating positive from negative needles. Snowden's crusade for privacy (Snowden, 2019) and the idea of encryption may demand a limit on the power of governments to use mass surveillance, but with a price totally ignored by those preaching for encryption-based privacy. Let me explain this point.

Mass surveillance in Western democracies, such as the USA, is to a large extent an overexaggerated issue, as for practical reasons the government has no interest in – and can do nothing with – the data it collects about John Doe and Miss Lucy from Texas (see Chapter 2). For Miss Lucy, the use of powerful encryption tools has no real or significant relevance. However, for crime organizations, violent political radicals organizing in militias, lone-wolf terrorists, insiders who seek to sell their companies' commercial secrets, human traffickers, and pedophiles, the new heaven proposed by Snowden's vision is a real asylum. Democracies will be much more vulnerable when citizens – regardless of their background, occupation, perversions, and motives – are given the ultimate freedom to use technologies reserved in the past to the most technologically sophisticated parts of the intelligence community. In contrast, non-democratic regimes will seldom be influenced by this vision of ultimate freedom, as any minimal attempt to use unauthorized means of communication or encryption will be used as evidence against the citizen. If we analyze the call for the ultimate level of encryption-based privacy, we may realize that any dogma, whether liberal or conservative, can be deadly to its citizens, as it represents the world in an oversimplistic, idealistic, and non-flexible manner. Remember the imaginary case of Dr. Adham Said, discussed in Chapter 1? Now imagine a "utopic" world formed along the lines of Snowden's vision, where Dr. Said has free access to full encryption in communicating his homemade knowledge about how to act against the decadent West. Is such a world a utopia or a dystopia? Should every insider be judged a whistleblower (positive) by their own testimony, or should they be judged as positive or negative on the basis of their actions and those actions' consequences?

In discussing the ethical issue, I would now like to summarize what I've proposed so far. I first tried to explain what a needle is and that a needle is not only a rare object but also one that is difficult to distinguish from its background (i.e. the haystack). The human needle is an emerging threat that proactively seeks to hide itself through using various strategies of camouflage, which we know from natural contexts. However, it is not the formed and "mature" needle that we are looking for, at least not as our main mission, but the evolving needle heading toward a tipping point where it may do some damage. The "edge" therefore lies in understanding the needle challenge in its full complexity. To help us gain such an edge, I proposed some negative and positive directions. On the negative side, I proposed to avoid, at least as a first step, the binary diagnostic approach that seeks to classify an object as a needle or not. On the positive side, I proposed a Bayesian approach that seeks to calibrate our prior belief that an object taken from a certain pool of "suspects" is a needle. This is not a one-shot game but a dynamic and incremental process where our prior beliefs may constantly change as relevant information (i.e. evidence) enters the system. To work within such a framework, I proposed that great emphasis should be placed on reducing the size of the haystack and using "impostors' clues," which may help us to differentiate *via negativa* between true needles and false needle. This process is performed within a general process of ranking individuals according to their risk factor the identification of the top-*k* objects, and their in-depth analysis or diagnosis. This phase of in-depth inspection is where balance of power is crucial and where the judicial system enters the picture to make sure the in-depth inspection is justified.

I then discussed the incremental approach, starting from screening and moving on to in-depth inspection and action under the title of prioritization-based action, where the process of screening and ranking the objects is accompanied by relevant actions. Such a ranked list of suspects may be dynamic and updated in real time. Moreover, the information we gather to form such a list comes from three different aspects, or dimensions, of the needle. First, we try to identify the "genetic signature," or the predisposition of each object to be a needle. This signature is relatively static and updated only when we learn something new about the essence of our object. The second dimension is context, which I defined in Chapter 9 as "the relational pattern through which the predisposition is expressed." Context is therefore the stratum on which the predisposition may express itself. A computer geek with a predisposition for misunderstanding social relations may be asked to work for the intelligence community in a hierarchical context requiring semi-military obedience to authority figures. This is a context that may invite a conflict with authority, and in such a context, the third dimension we should examine is contextual triggers, which I defined as features associated with a temporal outburst of the unwanted behavior. Our computer geek with an in-built difficulty understanding social relations and accepting authority may get into a conflict with their supervisor, whom they arrogantly dismiss as intellectually and technologically inferior. A threat to the self-value of our geek may turn them into a vengeful person who seeks to get even in order to prove their self-value. When screening such an object, we may notice that themes of revenge appear at an accelerating rate and that the troubling signals form a coherent picture of an individual moving toward a tipping point of which they are not always aware. Such a positive feedback loop of escalation may be eliminated in time when the appropriate intervention is available. Preventive steps should always be the first priority and they may surprisingly benefit the "needle" and their social circle (e.g. society or organization).

The discussion so far summarizes the main lessons derived from my analysis. However, it is highly important for me to re-emphasize the importance of approach over technique. Most engineering projects, in the sense of projects where we are developing *practical* technological solutions to specific challenges, require a flexible, pragmatic, and adaptive approach. In this context, one should not stick to theory, technique, or a well-formed protocol. Deep neural networks are the leading approach in AI, but they are not relevant in each and every context despite their appeal and buzzy nature. Getting out of the engineer's silo (see Chapter 6) seems to be the most important technique required by the educated engineer, not to say data scientist.

The poet John Keats coined the phrase "negative capability" to describe the capacity to experience uncertainties, mysteries, and doubts "without any irritable reaching after fact and reason" (Britannica, n.d.). This is not a required approach when we are dealing with relatively simple problems. However, when we are facing a real challenge, such an approach seems to be a must, at least as a kind of working attitude. I've titled this concluding chapter with a nice phrase from W. G. Sebald's novel in order to emphasize the complexity and uncertainty involved in the needle challenge. When we encounter this challenge – where what we see, at least at first, are just isolated lights in the abyss of ignorance – being able to adopt the right attitude seems to be the most important step before searching for the needle in the haystack.

REFERENCES

Britannica. (n.d.). Negative capability. Retrieved January 19, 2022, from https://www.britannica.com/art/negative-capability

Sebald, W. G. (1998). *The rings of Saturn*. London, UK: Harvill Press.

Snowden, E. (2019). *Permanent record*. New York, NY: Metropolitan Books.

Subject Index